The Great Legacy

'I have given them the glory that you gave me.'
John 17:22

Selwyn Hughes & Philip Greenslade
Revised and updated by Mick Brooks
FURTHER STUDY: IAN SEWTER

© CWR 2013. Dated text previously published as *Every Day with Jesus: The Legacy of Jesus* (March/April 2002) by CWR. This edition revised and updated for 2014 by Mick Brooks.

CWR, Waverley Abbey House, Waverley Lane, Farnham, Surrey GU9 8EP, UK
Tel: 01252 784700 Email: mail@cwr.org.uk
Registered Charity No. 294387. Registered Limited Company No. 1990308.

Cover image: Getty/Dorling Kindersley
Quiet Time image: unsplash/Alexander Shustov
Printed in England by Linney Print

MIX
Paper from
responsible sources
FSC® C015900

A word of introduction ...

'Legacy' is a word which can startle me; like a rabbit caught in headlights, momentarily frozen, I wrestle with my own insecurities, running my internal data file of those I have known whose 'legacy' has impacted people, communities, and even nations for good. Selwyn, who 'retired' in 2006, has left a truly amazing legacy which today is still changing lives around the world. Most people who become world-changers often didn't start out so. They began with being who they are in God, loving those around them in the way God wanted them to. One of our early vision statements at CWR was 'if we deepen, God will broaden'. In other words, if we concentrate on what God has put before us, focus on Him, His plans and purposes, He will in His good time and in His way take care of the rest ... I remind myself to rest and trust in Him. This issue explores the great legacy of Jesus, although these pages do not have the capacity to adequately outline what Jesus has put in place for mankind. It is staggering to consider the impact of the price paid for us and the promises made. I was reminded recently of perhaps Jesus' greatest gift: His presence. Ben Cantelon's song 'My Guardian' reminds us that God is before and beside us and will always find us if we wander. Can there be any greater gift?

I trust you will discover God's great love and presence afresh in these coming weeks as you discover more of the impact of the great legacy of Jesus.

Grace and peace for this Easter season.

Mick Brooks, Consulting Editor

Free small group resources to accompany this issue can be found at www.cwr.org.uk/extra. The *EDWJ* Facebook community is growing! To join the conversation visit www.facebook.com/edwjpage f

'Reading His will'

FOR READING & MEDITATION - JOHN 14:15-31
'Peace I leave with you; my peace I give you.' (v27)

Our theme in this issue is 'The Great Legacy', that is, the amazing things accomplished by Jesus that He left for us. What a person normally leaves behind in their last will and testament is their accumulated wealth and possessions to be distributed. But Jesus left behind no material possessions, no bank account, no houses or land. His legacy was of an altogether different kind. As we explore His legacy, so to speak, over these next two months, hopefully together we will appreciate more fully our inheritance in Christ Jesus.

Foremost among Jesus' bequests was His peace. *Shalom* (the Hebrew word which we interpret as 'peace') was the customary Jewish greeting and farewell, which no doubt for some had become a mere formality. But Jesus filled it with new meaning. His peace is different both in kind and in the way it is given from anything the world has to offer. It is not reliant on outward circumstances or absence of conflict. In fact, it flourishes in the midst of trouble. As Dr W.E. Sangster put it: 'Galilee in storm and Calvary in darkness set it off.' Jesus' serenity was born of confidence in His Father's goodness, trust in His Father's sovereignty, and surrender to His Father's will. What Jesus leaves is not a placebo to con the heart into being untroubled. It is the Messiah's peace, the *shalom* of God's kingdom established in the midst of strife. This is the peace Jesus bequeathed as a gift to His disciples on the verge of His departure to help dispel their fear.

No one has ever demonstrated such peace in the midst of trouble as did Jesus. His was a peace that didn't go to pieces. And that same peace can be yours, but first we need to be open to receiving.

FURTHER STUDY

Gen. 25:29-34;
Heb. 9:11-28,
12:16

1. How may we be like Esau?

2. What is our inheritance?

Heavenly Father, I know that peace is available. Help me open myself to its flow. I long for my inmost being to be held by peace. The surface may be disturbed but it's the depths that coun. Help me be secure there, dear Father. Amen.

Finding resolution

FOR READING & MEDITATION – JOHN 12:20-36

'Now my heart is troubled ... Father, glorify your name!' (vv27-28)

The peace that Jesus bequeathed to His disciples, as we saw yesterday, was not rooted in a life in idyllic surroundings far removed from the tension of human existence. On the contrary, the circumstances of Jesus' life were tumultuous. He experienced constant intrusions on His privacy, felt drained by the demands He faced, and knew the bleakness of sin and burden of need all round Him. He was misunderstood and on the receiving end of cutting criticism and unkind innuendo. He was in turns baffled by and betrayed by His followers.

FURTHER STUDY

Mark 4:35-41;
2 Pet. 2:7-9

1. How did the disciples find peace in a storm?

2. Why was Lot distressed?

Please notice, however, that He never sidestepped or avoided inner turmoil. 'Now my heart is troubled,' He confessed. The word chosen by John to describe this is used of the tossing waves of a turbulent sea! Jesus was 'churned up' on the inside. Though at one with His Father, He was at odds with a mutinous world, and He felt the contradiction in His own heart. In conventional terms, says Archbishop Rowan Williams, Jesus was a 'singularly unpeaceful person'.

Yet, as today's reading reveals to us, He immediately found a resolution for His lack of peace in the Father's love and in the Father's purpose for His life. There is no circumstance of trouble or affliction in which it is impossible to find the peace of glorifying God. We so often forget that. When your heart is churned up because you sense you are at odds with the world – the world that ultimately crucified Jesus – it is possible to sense an inner peace that comes from knowing that God's purposes will be fulfilled despite the negatives that shout at you from all directions. This is the peace which is one aspect of Jesus' legacy to us. How wonderful. How truly wonderful.

Yes, Father, it is wonderful that because Your peace is in my heart I can look at life and say: 'Do your worst or your best. I have peace, adequate peace, within.' I am so grateful. Blessed be Your name for ever. Amen.

Finding peace with God

FOR READING & MEDITATION - LUKE 2:1-14

'Glory to God in the highest, and on earth peace to men on whom his favour rests.' (v14)

The peace Jesus came to exemplify and to give was not peace 'as the world gives' (John 14:27). The peace that comes with Jesus, like Him, comes down from heaven to earth. There is nothing in the world as it is now, ravaged by sin, selfishness and war, that can produce lasting peace. The best that the world can give is a temporary oasis. Scripture says: 'There is no peace for the wicked' (Isa. 48:22). And why? Because perfect peace comes from adjustment to reality, and there can be no adjustment to reality without adjustment to God. A strife-torn earth needs a heaven sent peace. This is what is available in Jesus. The world has spun off its axis – the loving will of its Creator. Everything is now out of kilter. All things need realignment, reconciliation and restoration.

Critical to this is the re-establishment of God's glory as the chief priority in His world. When God's glory is reinstated as the hub around which all creation revolves then there will be peace on earth as there is in heaven. The birth of Jesus heralded the salvation that brings us peace. Peace between God and mankind, peace between us, peace within us – every dimension of this glorious, saving peace came to us as a gift of God's grace with the arrival of His Son, Jesus. No wonder the angelic choirs pulled out all the stops in praise of such a moment and such a favour.

Remember, however, that you cannot fully receive the peace *of* God until you have peace *with* God. If you have never received Jesus Christ into your life as Saviour and Lord then do so now. When you pray this prayer and mean it, you will be reorientated to reality. As you find peace *with* God you will soon find your soul flooded with the peace *of* God.

FURTHER STUDY

Rom. 5:1-11;
Col. 1:15-23

1. How can we have peace with God?

2. How were we enemies of God?

Heavenly Father, help me to be sure that my soul is at peace with You so that I can claim the peace that comes from You. I do so now. Save me, forgive my sins, come into my heart, and make me Your child. In Jesus' name I pray. Amen.

A heart at rest

FOR READING & MEDITATION - LUKE 7:36-50

'Jesus said to the woman, "Your faith has saved you; go in peace."'
(v50)

We ended yesterday with the thought that when we have peace *with* God we can know the peace *of* God. In measure, this is what happened to the woman in today's reading. She found peace for her troubled soul – a soul splintered by guilt and shame. It is difficult to say whether the woman had found peace prior to washing Jesus' feet or while she was engaged in that very act. Most likely it was the former. 'Go in peace,' is the parting word of Jesus to this woman who 'had lived a sinful life in that town' (v37).

FURTHER STUDY

Psa. 32:1-7;
Eph. 2:1-10

1. Describe the psalmist's experience.

2. How has grace transformed us?

Drawn to Jesus, with a prostitute's history behind her, she comes to lavish praise on Him for the transforming grace she has tasted. Simon, the Pharisee, is more constrained in his appreciation of Jesus. But, because she had been forgiven much, she loved much. The costly perfume was maybe used as one of the tricks of her trade. Maybe it was the only thing that remained from her previous life. Whether or not that was so, she gives it in a risky tribute to Jesus' grace.

The peace she found was the serenity of a sinner saved by Jesus' loving grace and acceptance. Her peace was the exhilarating wholeness of being accepted by a God of unconditional love and mercy. And notice that Jesus made the first and crucial move in restoring her to full status in the community of Israel. No longer would she sell her body; she had sold her soul once and for all to the Son of God. She could walk now with head held high.

Serenely she leaves the house, free from the abusive power of previous clients, free from the withering disdain of self-righteous people like Simon, free to take her place as a true member of God's people once again. There is no peace like the peace of sins forgiven.

O Father, how thankful I am for the peace of sins forgiven. My heart that once was hot and restless with feelings of guilt and shame is now at rest. I have been forgiven. All honour and glory be to Your precious Name. Amen.

CWR Ministry Events

PLEASE PRAY FOR THE TEAM

ATE	EVENT	PLACE	PRESENTER(S)
Mar	Transformed by the Presence of Jesus	Waverley Abbey House	Liz Babbs
Mar	Understanding Yourself: Understanding Others	WAH	Lynn and Andrew Penson
9 Mar	Preparation for Marriage	WAH	Lynette and Mick Brooks
Mar	Small Group Leader's Toolbox	WAH	Andy Peck
Mar	Women's Spring Day: Being a Secure Woman - in an Insecure World	Pilgrim Hall	Paula Buchel and Jeannette Barwick
-21 Mar	Introduction to Biblical Care and Counselling	WAH	Angie Coombes and team
3-30 Mar	Women's Weekend: Reaching for Jesus' Hand	WAH	Paula Buchel and Karen Case-Green
3 Mar	Helping Couples with Troubled Marriages	WAH	Heather and Ian Churchill
Apr	Christians @ Work: Working with Others	WAH	Beverley Shepherd
Apr	Passover Supper	WAH	Elizabeth Hodkinson
4 Apr	Developing Pastoral Care extra day	WAH	Philip Greenslade and Andy Peck
5 Apr	Counselling Enquirers' Event	WAH	
3 Apr	Helping Families Manage Change	WAH	Andre Radmall

lease also pray for students and tutors on our ongoing **BA in Counselling** programme
t Waverley and Pilgrim Hall and our **Certificate and Diploma of Christian Counselling**
nd **MA in Integrative Psychotherapy** held at London School of Theology.

or further details and a full list of CWR's courses, phone +44 (0)1252 784719
r visit the CWR website at **www.cwr.org.uk** Pilgrim Hall: **www.pilgrimhall.com**

The Prince of Peace

FOR READING & MEDITATION – LUKE 19:28-48

'If you, even you, had only known on this day what would bring you peace – but now it is hidden from your eyes.' (v42)

Everyone longs for peace, but sadly not everyone wants or understands the things that make for peace. Jerusalem in the time of Jesus wanted peace. It had settled for an uneasy alliance with the pagan Romans, and felt it could buy peace by compromise with an alien culture. A number of Jews, however, believed that they could make peace by armed revolt. Others felt they could achieve peace by turning their backs on the moral muddle and spiritual ambiguity, retreating to the desert to form monastic communities, which were considered holy and detached.

FURTHER STUDY

Isa. 9:1-7;
Jer. 6:9-16

1. What is God's promise?

2. Why did the people have no rest for their souls?

Today many people have a casual attitude to sex, mistaking sex for intimacy, then wonder why they struggle to find lasting peace in their relationships. They ignore God's commandments and are then surprised that society is so dysfunctional. They want peace but on their own terms and in their own way. But real peace eludes them.

The disciples seemed to relish the prospect of heaven's peace being offered to the city through the peaceful king riding symbolically into His capital city, not on a warhorse but on a donkey. But His opponents protested: 'We don't want this man to be our king' (compare v14). They wanted peace, but not the Prince of Peace. So, while friends rejoiced and critics found fault, Jesus wept that so many would miss His peace.

How Jesus must weep still as He sees individuals, families, and whole nations struggling to find peace but giving no thought to the Prince of Peace. As we said earlier, there can be no real peace without the ultimate realignment – the adjustment to reality, to God Himself. If He is not its source then circumstances or distress can easily push it over.

Lord Jesus Christ, master of time and tide and turmoil, help all to see that there can be no real peace in this universe unless the knee is bowed to the Prince of Peace. For Your own dear name's sake. Amen.

His peace – my peace

FOR READING & MEDITATION - JOHN 16:17-33
'I have told you these things, so that in me you may have peace.
In this world you will have trouble.' (v33)

What amazing words of reassurance these words of Jesus are. Martin Luther expressed this thought to his friend and fellow Reformer, Philipp Melanchthon: 'Such a saying as this is worthy to be carried from Rome to Jerusalem upon one's knees!' How extraordinary that the peace Jesus gives can coexist with pressure and even persecution. His peace stems from His victory, already won over sin and evil. He has overcome the world!

Once more we realise that when Jesus speaks of peace He is not talking of some feel-good factor enjoyable only in trouble-free times. This is a deeply rooted peace to be experienced in the heat of battle. We can discover tranquillity in the middle of trials, calm in the centre of crises. Such peace is the fruit of 'courage' (v33, translated 'take heart' in the NIV), which was exactly what Jesus encouraged the disciples to embrace when caught in the storm on Galilee (Mark 4:35-41). Jesus nowhere promises His followers a bed of roses. In fact, He foresees trouble ahead; conflict is inevitable if we follow Him. But because He has overcome, we can take courage. Because He is exultant, we can be too. When we are in Jesus then we have His peace flowing into our hearts.

FURTHER STUDY

Acts 16:14-34

1. How did Paul and Silas display peace in turmoil?

2. What was the result?

A traveller in the Arizona desert noticed a bird's nest hollowed out of a prickly cactus tree. The nest was surrounded by thorns, but among them a bird had hollowed out a place of security and peace. As he looked at the nest he said to himself: 'In the midst of a thorny environment I can find the same degree of peace that Jesus displayed in the midst of His thorny world. His peace is my peace.' However difficult or thorny a situation may be, Jesus' presence and power enables us to be calm.

Father, I am so thankful that the peace which flowed in Your Son's heart can be in mine also. Because I am in Him and He is in me there can be a total deliverance from peacelessness. I am deeply thankful. Amen.

Breathe on me ...

FOR READING & MEDITATION - JOHN 20:19-31

'... Jesus came and stood among them and said,
"Peace be with you!"' (v19)

Three times in this passage Jesus gives the salutation 'Peace be with you!' Prior to going to the cross Jesus promised His disciples that He would leave them with His peace and now, on the other side of Calvary, He reaffirms that fact. Some might consider that His 'Peace be with you' was merely the conventional greeting. Perhaps. But its repetition would surely have prompted the disciples to remember His earlier promise to bequeath them His own distinctive peace.

As well as being a word commonly used in conversation, *shalom* was also the term that summed up the all-embracing wellbeing that would characterise God's people in the final Messianic kingdom of God. George Beasley-Murray, a noted New Testament scholar and one-time principal of Spurgeon's College, wrote this in his commentary on John's Gospel: '*Shalom* on Easter evening is the equivalent of "It is finished" on the cross, for the peace of reconciliation and the life from God is now imparted.'

FURTHER STUDY

Acts 7:54-60,
27:20-26

1. What gave Stephen a sense of peace?

2. What gave Paul hope and peace?

If, like the disciples, you feel hemmed in by closed doors of fear at the moment, let the words of Jesus speak peace to your anxious heart. Reflect as they did, in wonder at His scarred hands and side, and rekindle your joy in the sight of your Saviour. Beyond death, the risen One bestows a legacy of peace and life. Hear again the triumphant declaration which we considered yesterday: 'I have overcome the world' (John 16:33). Within that world which He has overcome is included every single difficulty you have to meet in your life. Jesus breathed peace to His bewildered and confused disciples. If your heart is troubled He is waiting to do the same for you right now.

Lord Jesus Christ, breathe upon my waiting heart the gift I long to receive – the gift of peace. Grant that I might feel from this moment until the day I die peace and adequacy and power – the peace of Your presence deep within. Amen.

Level ground

FOR READING & MEDITATION - EPHESIANS 2:11-22

'For he himself is our peace, who has made the two one and has destroyed the barrier' (v14)

We venture now outside the Gospels to ponder Paul's celebration of Jesus' accomplishment and the peace that comes through the cross. The Romans achieved peace in the ancient world – the *pax Romana* – by force of arms and cruel conquest. They suppressed rebellion by bloodshed and violence. The peace of the Roman Empire, a sign of oppression and punishment, was established on the crosses it erected. But the peace which Jesus Christ leaves behind is the peace that comes from the very same cross. Though erected by the Romans, Jesus' cross became the place from which the greatest peace the world has ever known was transmitted – the peace of God.

Jesus' death was a costly act of peacemaking. We who were alienated rebels, caught, as someone has said, 'with the weapons of insurrection in our hands', have been reconciled to a holy God by the death of His Son. Gentiles who were excluded from the spiritual privileges granted to Israel, and 'foreigners to the covenants of the promise' (v12), have been brought near by Christ's cross, says Paul.

FURTHER STUDY

Gal. 3:26-29;
Col. 3:7-17

1. What barriers has Christ broken down?

2. What is our calling?

In a world of cultural conflict and discrimination, Christ Himself is our peace. The ground is level at the foot of His cross. In Him every ungodly wall is demolished, every prideful barrier broken down. Wherever His atoning death is preached, owned, and embraced, peace breaks out. Reconciled to God and to each other, the recipients of His peace share equal access to their Father God and join in heartfelt praise. There is no malice or mutual hate, no bitter feud or long-standing antagonism that cannot in the end be absorbed and neutralised by the transforming love of Jesus' cross. If that's not worth a shout of Hallelujah then nothing is.

My Father and my God, how can I sufficiently thank You for enduring the pain of the cross so that I might find everlasting peace? Grant that all who may come in touch with me this day may sense this peace in my heart. In Jesus' name. Amen.

Perfect trust – perfect peace

FOR READING & MEDITATION – ISAIAH 26:1–6

'You will keep in perfect peace him whose mind is steadfast, because he trusts in you.' (v3)

This powerful verse from the Old Testament shows us the need for a conscious centring of our minds on God. He is not the place of occasional reference; He is the centre of our world, love and loyalty. There can be little doubt that this is the way Jesus lived. We only have to observe Him as He walks through the pages of the Gospels to see that His heart and mind were continually fixed on God. But not only must our minds be focused on God; as the text says, there is a need also for trust. Jesus' trust in His Father's love and purposes was perfect, and so He was able to receive and enjoy perfect peace.

The consequences of a lack of trust in God are seen in these lines by W.B. Yeats:

FURTHER STUDY

Psa. 37:1-11;
1 Tim. 6:6-19

1. Who will enjoy great peace?

2. Why may some people not experience peace?

Things fall apart, the centre cannot hold,
Mere anarchy is loosed upon the world,
The best lack all conviction, while the worst,
Are full of passionate intensity.

Things fall apart because the centre cannot hold, says Yeats. This always happens when the centre is not God Himself.

A large number of people think the acquisition of things will help stave off anxiety, but often find it increases it. At a time when the prescription of mood enhancing drugs is at an all time high, it is sad that so many are ill prepared for the day that lies ahead because they have not had a restorative sleep. Jesus, it appears, had no trouble sleeping. On one occasion He slept through a storm (Matt. 8:24)! Let Him breathe His peace deep into your heart and you too will be able to sleep through every 'storm'.

Father, I see more clearly than ever that You are desirous of giving deep inner peace. Help me open myself to Your healing peace. May my mind be fixed on You and not on my troubles. In Jesus' name. Amen.

The seed of faith, with love ...

... from you, to people in need, both at home and around the world who seek – like you – the guidance to live their everyday lives as God wills.

Jesus said, 'The kingdom of heaven is like a mustard seed, which a man took and planted in his field. Though it is the smallest of all your seeds, yet when it grows ... becomes a tree, so that birds of the air come and perch in its branches' (Matt. 13:31-32).

Please help CWR to invest in the lives of others and root themselves in God's Word and love.

Please fill in the 'Gift to CWR' section on the order form at the back of this publication, completing the Gift Aid declaration if appropriate.

How to receive peace

FOR READING & MEDITATION - PHILIPPIANS 4:1-9

'And the peace of God, which transcends all understanding,
will guard your hearts and your minds ' (v.7)

Since Jesus has bequeathed His peace to us the question we must ask ourselves is this: How do we receive it? One commentator makes this suggestion: 'Stand in the way of allowing peace to invade you. Peace is knocking at the door. Lift the latch and let peace come in.' Perhaps you are thinking to yourself: 'That's easy to say but not so easy to do.' Here is one man's testimony as to how he learned to open himself to the peace which Jesus promises to give.

'I was afraid to live and afraid to die. I feared people. I feared everything. I feared getting up in the morning and I feared going to bed in the evening. One night I read the words of Jesus in John 20 when He appeared to the disciples, breathed on them and said: "Peace be with you!" It came home to me like a bolt out of the blue that all I had to do was release my fears to Christ and stand in the place where He could breathe His peace into my heart. The mistake I had been making was that I wanted God's peace to come into me before I would release my fears. He showed me that when I released my fears – surrendered them to Him – then peace would be the result. Peace could not come in when I clung to my fears. Surrendering them made an opening for peace to rule in my heart. And it did. Oh, how it did!'

FURTHER STUDY

Psa. 119:161-168;
Col. 3:5-15

1. Who has great peace?

2. How do we put off fear and put on peace?

John Calvin, the Reformer, said on one occasion: 'God reduced my mind to a teachable frame.' When your mind is in 'a teachable frame' you are receptive and willing to surrender all your fears into Jesus' hands. And when you put everything in His hands and are willing to open your heart fully to Him then peace is the inevitable result. Jesus wills His peace to you. Now accept the will that wills your peace.

Lord Jesus Christ, I hand over all my fears into Your hands. No longer will I hold on to them, nurse them or indulge them. They are Yours. Now I receive Your perfect peace. Breathe it into me as You breathed it into Your disciples. Amen.

Washing of the feet

FOR READING & MEDITATION – JOHN 13:1-17

'Now that you know these things, you will be blessed if you do them.'
(v.17)

We move on now to consider another of Christ's precious legacies: His example. There are so many wonderful ways in which He has set us an example, but over the coming days we will have to be content with just highlighting a few. Take this incident, recorded in today's reading. In washing His disciples' feet, Jesus was demonstrating one of the greatest examples of His inner peace and humility.

There are many who believe that when Jesus said to His disciples, 'You also should wash one another's feet' (v14), He meant that every one of His followers throughout the ages should literally practise this ritual. It is debatable whether or not this is so, though multitudes of Christians in many parts of the world still continue this practice. And some of the services in which this is done are very moving and meaningful indeed. However, following Jesus' example has more to do with the practice of humility, so that we are Christlike in the way we speak and act and react.

But someone might object and say: 'Jesus is God, and everything is easy for God. With us, however, frail and human as we are, it is quite different.' Theologian Douglas Webster puts it well when he says: 'It is a terrible irony when Christians excuse their failure to become like Jesus by using the excuse that His deity makes Him exceptional.' The spirit He demonstrated can be our spirit if we allow Him to preside and reside within us. In fact because, uniquely, He humbled Himself to death to save us, everything about His spirit is relevant to our lives. His story is to be our story in the sense that our actions are to be threaded with humility – as were His.

FURTHER STUDY

Matt. 11:28-30;
Phil. 2:5-11

1. Consider the character of Christ.

2. What did Jesus give up?

O Father, grant that Your Son's spirit may invade me and pervade me so that my attitude to others will be the same as Your Son's attitude to me. I am at the feet of the Man who washes feet. Make me a willing servant. In Jesus' name. Amen.

The root of humility

FOR READING & MEDITATION - JOHN 13:1-17

'... he poured water into a basin and began to wash his disciples'
feet, drying them with the towel' (v5)

So amazing and astonishing is this passage that we must
spend another day considering it. The root of Jesus'
astonishing humility lay in His sense of total security and
understanding about who He was. Secure in the knowledge
of His origin (that He had come from God), His destiny
(and was returning to God), and His God-given authority
(the Father had put all things under His power), He could
without embarrassment or loss of face bend to wash His
disciples' feet. Free from the incessant demand to prove
Himself, free from the pressure to keep up appearances, He
was free to humble Himself for His Father's glory
and His friends' needs. Jesus knew who He was
because He knew whose He was, and, confident
of His place in God, He was able to take a towel
and wash the disciples' feet.

**FURTHER
STUDY**

Mark 10:35-45;
1 Cor. 15:9-11;
1 Tim. 1:12-17

1. What
did Jesus
explain about
greatness?

2. How did the
great apostle
Paul view
himself?

This was not self-belittlement – as much of what
we often call humility is – but a consciousness of
greatness. You see, the consciousness of greatness
is the secret of humility. The small dare not be
humble; it would be too threatening for them. But
Jesus' greatness was rooted in God, and being in
God made Him great – and humble. Dr E. Stanley
Jones said that Jesus was: 'Great because humble
and humble because great.' Only 'in Him' can
we be set free from the destructive insecurity
that makes us either over-assert ourselves against our
neighbour or degrade ourselves in self-loathing and shame.

Humility is possible to those whose lives have been re-
rooted in the love of God in Christ. If your past and your
future and your present times are in God's hands then you
will experience true greatness. It will not devalue you to
take a towel and wash feet. As the Master, so the servant.

**Father, I accept that the source of humility is the consciousness
of greatness. Help me see that my position is in God, not in
myself, and from that position help me minister in true humility
to others. In Jesus' name. Amen.**

Followership

'If anyone would come after me, he must deny himself and take up his cross and follow me.' (v34)

We continue reflecting on the fact that one of Jesus' most precious legacies to us is His example. 'Follow me,' He said over and over again to the men and women of His day. Christians are so familiar with these words that we are apt to overlook the astounding claim that lies behind them. Who is this person who sets Himself up as the arbiter of human destiny? Who is this who sets the example for all men and women to aspire to? It is none other than God's Son, the Creator of all things (Col. 1:16).

The poet Charles Lamb once said: 'If Shakespeare were to come into the room we would all rise to meet him, but if that Other Person were to come into the room we would all fall down and kiss the hem of His garment.' What a wonderful example He is. All kinds of people warmed to His appeal. Tough fishermen, women of the streets, Roman soldiers, religious leaders, civil servants – they were all drawn by His charisma.

FURTHER STUDY

Luke 18:18-30; John 6:60-69

1. Why did the ruler not follow Christ?

2. Contrast 'many disciples' and the Twelve.

Two ways lie open before us: the way of the self-directed life, and the way set by Jesus Christ. He calls us to a life of faith; of giving up our self-dependence, turning to Him and living a life of God-dependence and trust. We take up our cross not when we put up with minor inconveniences such as grumpy relatives or bad weather but when we choose, on a daily basis, to forego self-interest in order to follow His leadership in living. Interestingly, and most importantly, we discover that we don't lose our true selves this way; paradoxically, we find out who we really are only as we relate to Him. As we have said before, we don't know who we are until we know whose we are. It is in belonging to Christ and following Him that we discover our real identity and our real destiny.

Lord Jesus Christ, I see so clearly that the more I know You the more I know myself. In Your light I see light. My heart therefore cries: 'Lead on, dear Saviour. I will follow You wherever You go.' Amen.

Following - no easy option

FOR READING & MEDITATION - MATTHEW 10:24-42

'A student is not above his teacher, nor a servant above his master.'
(v24)

One of Matthew's aims in writing his Gospel was to encourage Christians facing hardship and experiencing resistance in their witness of Jesus. But opposition is only to be expected, says Matthew; Jesus Himself encountered hostility throughout His ministry.

It is, of course, somewhat unnerving that the call to follow Jesus will just about always involve suffering in some form or another, but that fact needs to be understood. Jesus endured much misunderstanding and abuse – and so will we. He was even accused on one occasion of being satanic, of being inspired by 'Beelzebub' (Matt. 12:24)! Even in 'tolerant' countries Christians who affirm their belief in the Bible are often looked down on patronisingly, their testimony mocked as outdated, their joy disdainfully dismissed as 'happy-clappy'. But our reading reminds us that no servant is above his master. Obvious success and outward approval are no criteria of faithfulness, as the example of Jesus shows. It is, in fact, our highest privilege to be treated as He was treated. What matters to the faithful servant is to be like the Master and to be acknowledged by Him in the Father's presence (v32).

FURTHER STUDY

Luke 9:57-62, 14:25-35

1. What did Jesus explain?

2. Explain how we carry our cross.

Above all, we can be thankful for the realism of Jesus. 'Jesus is not expansive about the possibilities of Christian mission,' says Dale Bruner. 'He knows that His mission is a rugged minority movement, a tough, divisive affair, and He prefers to make it clear rather than give false hopes.' Following the example of Jesus is no easy option but a challenging vocation. Yet how can we keep from not following Him? In the words of one hymn writer: 'It is the path the Master trod, should not the servant tread it still?'

My Father and my God, how delighted I am that my feet have found the path down which Your own Son walked, the path that leads at last to glory. Knowing what I know, I cannot but follow. Thank You my Father. Amen.

Both sides of Easter

FOR READING & MEDITATION - 1 PETER 2:13-25

'... Christ suffered for you, leaving you an example, that you should follow in his steps.' (v21)

Many notable and mature Christian commentators have observed that many Christians have an uneasy relationship with the Gospels. They tend to focus more on the letters of the apostles than they do on the four Gospels because they want to live – and quite rightly – in a post-Easter experience. But there is a danger of speed-reading the events leading up to the crucifixion and regarding them as unimportant to us. If we are not careful, this can lead us to think that Jesus did all the suffering and dying and we do all the living and triumphing.

If we read the writings of the apostles carefully, however, we soon discern that they lived on both sides of Easter and will have none of this one-sided discipleship. Peter, like Paul, revels in the salvation and victory that have been won for us by the shedding of the uniquely precious blood of the Lamb of God. Yet these two apostles also know that the resurrection has not cancelled out the cross but endorsed it as the God-honouring way to live. To follow in Jesus' footsteps, then, will at times be to endure hardship and injustice and even persecution. And in following His example we also learn the lesson and example from Him of reacting as He reacted, not answering spite with malice, not responding to insults by seeking revenge. Instead we entrust ourselves, as Jesus did, to the God who judges justly.

Peter's words were first addressed to Christians who were slaves, but who could shine with Christlikeness even when unjustly treated by oppressive masters. Many Christians today are unjustly treated for their faith. But if first-century slaves can exemplify Jesus then surely we can!

FURTHER STUDY

2 Cor. 11:22-33;
1 Pet. 4:12-19

1. What was Paul's experience of Christianity?

2. What was Peter's warning and advice?

O Father, forgive me I pray if I have been a one-sided disciple rejoicing in the victory of Your Son's resurrection but forgetting that I too have a cross to carry. I want to live on both sides of Easter. Please help me my Father. Amen.

The imitation of Christ

FOR READING & MEDITATION - 1 CORINTHIANS 10:23-11:1

'Follow my example, as I follow the example of Christ.' (11:1)

Paul is not being immodest in urging us to follow his example as he followed the example of Christ. Quite the reverse. In fact, he is countering the Corinthian fascination with showy and self-regarding leaders who sought to gain a following in Corinth whatever the integrity of their lifestyle. Paul offers himself as a model *only in so far as he models Christ*.

One reason why Paul fought so fiercely for his apostolic reputation was because he believed that the gospel he preached was to be exemplified in the messengers. The way in which Paul imitated Christ is clear from the immediate context. Paul lived *for the glory of God and the good of others*. We *should* relish our freedom in Christ, Paul affirms. Jesus was radically free, scandalising strict religious opinion by eating with notorious sinners and calling no type of food unclean. But His freedom was not self-indulgence. As whatever Jesus did was for the glory of His Father and the saving good of others so Paul similarly looks out not for his own interests but the interests of others (vv24, 33), and urges that everything be done for the glory of God (v31). And as Jesus lived and died to save others so all that we do should be with their salvation in view (v33).

FURTHER STUDY

Eph. 4:1-6;
Phil. 2:1-4

1. What was Paul's challenge?

2. What should be our chief concern?

But what about our relationships with those who are already saved – our brothers and sisters in Christ? In those grey areas where Christians find that they disagree then those who model themselves on Christ will want to apply the example of the cross and seek to disagree agreeably. If we had uppermost in mind the interests of others whenever we discussed our disagreements, what a different place the Church of Jesus Christ would be.

Father, help me to model myself on Your Son and on the apostle Paul and do everything by the example of the cross. May I seek Your glory in everything, even in my genuine disagreements with others in Your body. In Jesus' name. Amen.

Our willingness, His power

FOR READING & MEDITATION - PHILIPPIANS 2:5-11

'Your attitude should be the same as that of Christ Jesus' (v5)

So amazing is this portrait of Jesus that it seems incredible that Paul is offering it as a model of Christlike behaviour for us to follow. This magnificent hymn to the humbled and exalted Christ is such a celebration of salvation that we may miss Paul's purpose in quoting it. He is seeking here to address disunity in the Philippian church caused by pride. To deal with it he urges his Philippian friends to 'let this mind be in you, which was also in Christ Jesus' (v5, AV). In other words, the 'hymn' is both a doctrinal celebration and an ethical appeal. Glory in Christ Jesus and then go and do as He did, is his point.

But this is not an appeal to imitate Jesus on our own and out of our own resources. Rather, by the strength of His saving grace working in us and in the community of faith, and through mutual love, we may learn to be like Him. One commentator, Gerald Hawthorne, notes that there is a hint as to the source of the power by which we can achieve this high goal of imitation in the expression 'in Christ Jesus' (v5, AV). 'The call to imitate Christ Jesus,' he says, 'is made possible by the power of the living, exalted Christ who is present and at work within the lives of believers through the work of His Holy Spirit.'

Jesus' example is not an impossible ideal because it comes with His empowerment! In other words, not only does He lift the challenge to almost unbelievable heights but He also provides the power by which we can reach up to it. He asks nothing of us except our willingness. We supply the willingness; He supplies the power. We need never fear God's challenges are beyond us; they are beyond us only if we are unwilling to avail ourselves of His power.

FURTHER STUDY

1 Cor. 4:10-17; Gal. 5:13-26

1. How did Paul follow Christ?

2. How can we follow Christ?

O Father, help me drop my anchor into the depths of this reassuring and encouraging revelation. You do not expect me to depend on my own strength alone to live up to Your standards, but to avail myself of Yours. Thank You my Father. Amen.

'Fully human, fully alive'

FOR READING & MEDITATION - ROMANS 8:28-39

'For those God foreknew he also predestined to be conformed to the likeness of his Son' (v29)

In this memorable passage Paul's words set the idea of the example of Jesus on the largest possible scale. He is illustrating the fact that Jesus Christ is the template to which God is working in transforming our lives. John Stott has pithily said: 'If we had to sum up in a single brief sentence what life is all about, why Jesus Christ came into this world to live and die and rise, and what God is up to in the long-drawn-out historical process … it would be difficult to find a more succinct explanation than this: *God is making human beings more human by making them more like Christ.*' The goal of all that God has done and is doing in order to save us and bring us to glory is to make us like Jesus. Conformity to Jesus is the final good to which the Spirit is working as He weaves God's sovereign purpose into the diverse circumstances of our lives.

FURTHER STUDY

Acts 11:19-26;
1 Cor. 15:45-57

1. What was special about the believers at Antioch?

2. How will we be like Jesus?

This, of course, does not mean that every man – least of all every woman – will end up being a thirty-three-year-old Jewish man! No individuality will ever be lost in becoming like Jesus. The question is often asked: 'What does a truly human life look like?' The answer is: 'Jesus.' When we look at Jesus we can say: the truly human life looks like that! He is God's perfect man. If, as Irenaeus said, 'The glory of God is a human being fully alive', then we know that the example of Jesus is not an ideal that mocks our best efforts but the final glory to which God will bring His family of sons and daughters.

John Stott's statement that God is making human beings more human by making them more like Christ is well worth pondering. The more like Jesus you become the more human you will be – and the more 'fully alive'.

Gracious Father, help me day by day to become more and more like Jesus, for I see the more like Him I am the more alive I will be. I want this 'aliveness' not just for myself but that I might share it with others. In Jesus' name. Amen.

Our full focus

FOR READING & MEDITATION - HEBREWS 12:1-11

'Let us fix our eyes on Jesus, the author and perfecter of our faith'
(v2)

Here, in the passage before us today, the writer, endeavouring to encourage and motivate his readers to persist under pressure, presents Jesus as the unforgettable example of persevering faith. The way Jesus endured hostility from those opposed to God's saving plan provides an example for the beleaguered Christians to whom the letter is addressed.

Stirred by the examples of Old Testament heroes of faith (see Hebrews 11), we can be even more stirred by a fresh vision of Jesus, the supreme exponent of faith. He is the pioneer of faith who leads us on to show us the way. He is our champion in faith who goes out ahead of us to confront the evil we face. He endures so that we may endure. He despised the shame of crucifixion so that we may disdain the scorn of being His followers. With the dispirited readers of Hebrews we are called to fix our attention on Him with undistracted concentration. Remember and recall His focus on the future joy of God's welcome and approval. Consider His bleeding feet that trod the path of victory, and take heart.

A hymn by Thomas Toke Lynch springs to mind:

FURTHER STUDY

John 20:10-18; Heb. 3:1-6

1. What was Mary's problem?

2. How do we 'fix our eyes' on Jesus?

> I have a captain, and the heart
> Of every private man
> Has drunk in valour from His eyes,
> Since first the war began.
> He is most merciful in fight,
> And of His scars a single sight
> The embers of our failing might
> Into a flame can fan.

What an example! What a legacy! What a vision!

O Father, help me draw my regular encouragement not merely from books or even from these daily notes but from fixing my eyes on Jesus. I will glance at other things that bring me encouragement but I want my gaze to be fully on Him. Amen.

Doing good

FOR READING & MEDITATION – LUKE 6:27-36

'Love your enemies, do good to those who hate you' (v27)

Another example Jesus set for us is the example of doing good. In the text before us today Jesus emphasised the fact that the true children of God delight in doing good – even to those who are their enemies. This was not just something Jesus preached; it was something He practised also. Years later, after Jesus had risen from the dead and returned to heaven, the apostle Peter said of Him: 'He went around doing good and healing all who were under the power of the devil, because God was with him' (Acts 10:38).

Nowadays, of course, 'do-gooder' is virtually a term of abuse. The phrase conjures up a picture of someone self-righteous and holier-than-thou who is patronising and generally irritating. But Jesus is a most glorious exception to that. His *modus operandi* marks Him out as the heaven-sent Saviour who, uniquely and humbly and self-sacrificially, 'went around doing good … because God was with him'.

FURTHER STUDY

Luke 22:47-51;
Titus 3:3-8

1. How did Jesus 'walk his talk'?

2. To what should we be devoted?

It is said that a man's works live after him. This was never more true than of Jesus. The Gospel writers were spoiled for choice in recording the evidence left by His miracles and mighty works. The whole world, John says, would not be big enough to house all the books that would need to be written as testimony to what Jesus did (John 21:25). Matthew, Mark, Luke and John, therefore, give us only a small selection of all the amazing things Jesus did. We might love to know more. But there is a point to their restraint. Their aim is not to dazzle us with supernatural special effects but move us to faith. They want us not to be bemused but to believe. And not only believe but follow the example Jesus has set for us. Have you done something good for someone lately?

O Father, forgive me if I am more taken up with the theory of the Christian life than its practice. Help me do something good for someone today. And not just today but every day. In Jesus' name I pray. Amen.

FOR READING & MEDITATION – JOHN 5:1-47

'... whatever the Father does the Son also does.' (v19)

Even the most casual reader cannot help but be impressed with the number of good works in which Jesus was involved when He was on earth. Lepers were touched and made whole, the blind given their sight, cripples walked again, water turned into wine, and a small boy's lunch made a feast for a multitude. We could go on.

But pause to ponder how the Gospel writers describe this evidence. Jesus' deeds are called *mighty works* (eg Matt. 11:20, 21, 23, KJV) – outpourings of divine energy, testifying how powerfully God was at work in Jesus. They are described as *acts of compassion* (eg Matt. 14:14) – the overflow of God's mercy and passionate desire to set a broken world right. Above all, they are to be read as *signs* (eg John 20:30) – pointing to the glorious reality of the kingdom of God which arrived in and through Jesus.

The reason why Jesus was able to do good can be found in today's reading. Jesus Christ was not interested in self-promotion but in 'finishing' what His Father had started! Jesus worked only where He saw His Father working and then only to round off what the Father had begun. What a stunning fact to face. Before setting out to do God's work we would be wise to prayerfully discern what God is doing and where He is doing it and then to do it with Him. How many times have we knocked on doors which God was not opening and then been surprised when we have stumbled on one which He was? Many sick were lying at the pool of the Bethesda that day, but in His mysterious sovereignty God was actively working only in one man. To him Jesus gravitated, speaking the word that completed the life-giving circuit through which God's power flowed.

FURTHER STUDY

1 Sam. 16:1-13;
1 Chron. 14:8-17

1. Why do we need to find out what God is doing?

2. Why did David use different strategies in battle?

Loving heavenly Father, give me, I pray, the wisdom and insight to knock on the doors that You want opened. Help me to follow Your guidance in everything and be sensitive to Your perfect will. In Jesus' name. Amen.

Come on this journey of
40 Days with Jesus

Dave Smith
Senior Pastor of
KingsGate Community
Church

THE CONCEPT
Dave Smith delves into the Gospels' accounts of the 40 day period after Jesus' resurrection and draws on 6 encounters where key biblical figures are transformed by our Saviour – encounters which can teach us much about our identity in Christ, and God's desire to empower us to live life as He intended.

THE VISION
As Senior Pastor of KingsGate Community Church in Peterborough, Dave led the church through his *40 Days with Jesus* series. It began on Easter Sunday with the celebration of the resurrection, and in the subsequent 6 weeks, Dave focused on Jesus' appearances to Mary, Peter and the disciples in the upper room and on the Emmaus road. His prayer was, and still is, that everyone hearing of these encounters would have their faith strengthened, their love deepened and their hope increased.

THE IMPACT
'The impact was tremendous. Our Sunday numbers for the 40 days were considerably up on normal, and the number of first-time responders and people re-committing their lives to Christ noticeably increased, too. In addition, existing Christians seemed to love the focus on Christ and having new encounters with Him!' (Dave Smith)

FOR YOU

Now you can apply the 40 day journey to your own life.
Dave has worked with CWR to make *40 Days with Jesus*
available for you and your church or small group. We
are passionate about churches learning together, so
as well as reading the 40 day devotional, groups and
individuals will have **free access to online sermon
outlines, small group discussions with short video
teachings and study guides, all created by Dave Smith.**

Go on this journey together and discover how these
encounters still have power to change lives today.

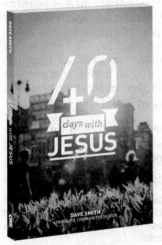

To purchase a copy priced at £6.99
(or £4.99 for orders of 10 or more
copies) use the order form at the
back of these notes, visit
www.cwr.org.uk/store or a
Christian bookshop.

Doing before teaching

FOR READING & MEDITATION - ACTS 1:1-11

'In my former book, Theophilus, I wrote about all that Jesus began to do and to teach' (v1)

Luke begins what we call 'The Acts of the Apostles' by referring to the fact that the Gospel he had written was all about what 'Jesus began to do and to teach'. Notice the way this part of the sentence is formed: 'all that Jesus began to *do* and to teach'. Christ's ministry consisted not just of teaching but of *doing* and teaching. The teaching was the unfolding of a doing, something that was operative within Himself. He taught nothing that He did not practise.

This gave His words authority and power. Luke, in his Gospel, says of Him: 'All the people were amazed and said to each other, "What is this teaching? With authority and power he gives orders to evil spirits and they come out!"' (Luke 4:36). Others quoted authorities, but when Jesus spoke He spoke with the authority of His own life behind everything He said. Jesus' teaching was powerful not just because of the things He said but because of the added authority He gave to everything He uttered – a power which came from His inner integrity and beauty of living. People didn't merely hear the Word – they saw it. The message was verbal but also vibrant in every part of His being. His deeds and His words blended together like the words and music of a song. Dr E. Stanley Jones said of Him: 'He was so truthful that He was Truth, so loving that He was Love, so good that He was Goodness, so morally beautiful that He was Beauty, so excellent in living that He was Life, so godlike that He was God.'

Jesus' teaching was not something imposed on life but exposed from it. That is why He is not a signpost pointing to the way; He is the way. And to follow Him is to find oneself on the way.

FURTHER STUDY

Matt. 11:1-5;
Luke 4:14-22

1. What was Jesus' answer to John's question?

2. What was Jesus' manifesto?

O God, how easy it is to focus more on teaching than doing. I sense the challenge of all this. Help me keep these things in balance so that it may be said also of me that my teaching arises from my doing. In Jesus' name. Amen.

Jesus - perfect in all things

FOR READING & MEDITATION - JOHN 8:42-47

'If I am telling the truth, why don't you believe me?' (v46)

Yesterday we saw that Luke began what we call 'The Acts of the Apostles' (which may more correctly be 'The Acts of Jesus through the Apostles') by referring to the fact that in his Gospel he had written 'about all that Jesus began to *do* and to teach' (Acts 1:1). The order, we said, is important - first doing, then teaching. Jesus' examples of doing and teaching were one; crack the shell of His outer deeds and you see the kernel of eternal meanings.

A missionary to India tells of how he looked at the frescoes on the walls of a temple - images of gods doing all kinds of foolish things - and then asked the keeper of the temple: 'Do these frescoes on the walls help you worship your gods?' The man replied: 'You have to be very strong if you come to this temple otherwise you will go and do what the gods do.' Revealing, don't you agree?

When we look at Jesus Christ we never feel that divine qualities are imposed on Him, but rather exposed out of Him. They come from within. We can detect at once what is imposed on Him by later centuries and what is exposed out of Him. One is artificial, the other is artesian. For example, a manuscript was discovered years ago in Ethiopia which was purported to be 'The Gospel of Thomas'. It has in it this sentence: 'Peter said to Jesus, "Send Mary away for it is not befitting that a woman should inherit eternal life along with the men." "No," said Jesus, "she need not go away. I will turn her into a male and she can therefore inherit eternal life."' That is what happens when man imposes divine qualities on Jesus - he produces a twisted, distorted truth. How thankful we ought to be for the wonder and veracity of the New Testament.

FURTHER STUDY

Luke 1:1-4; John 14:1-11

1. Why should we believe in the New Testament?

2. Why should we believe in Jesus?

Lord, the more I compare You with others, the more wondrous You are in my eyes. Your perfection, however, does not paralyse me; it awakens me, inspires me, beckons me on. Help me be more like You. For Your own dear name's sake. Amen.

Motives are everything

FOR READING & MEDITATION - GALATIANS 6:1-10

'... let us do good to all people, especially to those who belong to the family of believers.' (v10)

We continue reflecting on the example of Jesus, of whom it was said: 'He went around doing good and healing all who were under the power of the devil' (Acts 10:38). In the text before us today the apostle Paul reminds us that we are to 'do good to all people, especially to those who belong to the family of believers'. As we follow Jesus' example and do good to others we must be careful that we do so in the spirit of Jesus. Motives, it has been said, are everything. Jesus' motive in doing good was not to impress people with His kindness of heart but because it was His very nature. Here's a searching word: 'Anyone, then, who knows the good he ought to do and doesn't do it, sins' (James 4:17). As someone has said: 'The right thing to do is always the right thing to do.'

FURTHER STUDY

Matt. 15:29-38;
James 2:14-18;
1 John 3:16-18

1. What motivated Jesus?

2. What is a test of our faith?

Earlier we mentioned the fact that the term 'do-gooder' is virtually a term of abuse because it conjures up a picture of someone who is self-righteous and has a holier-than-thou attitude. However, doing good does not make us do-gooders – people who do good primarily to meet some need in themselves. Tony Campolo, an American speaker and author, believes that when we do good we should strive as far as possible to remain anonymous. For instance, he says that Christian young people who go to a needy home at Christmas, sing carols, and present a food package to the people living there are going about matters in the wrong way. They should, he says, leave the package at the door with a note: 'God loves you and sent you this.' He has a point. Jesus' good works flowed out of a heart that was over-flowing with compassion and a desire to set a sick and broken world right. What an example. What a legacy.

Father, show me how to do good without being a do-gooder. May my motive be to honour and glorify Your name. When I stumble over this then help me stumble to my knees for I see that I have much to learn. In Jesus' name. Amen.

The feel of consistency

FOR READING & MEDITATION - MATTHEW 10:24-33

'There is nothing concealed that will not be disclosed, or hidden that will not be made known.' (v26)

Today we move on to consider the second part of the phrase we have been considering: 'all that Jesus began to do and to teach' (Acts 1:1). First doing and then teaching was mentioned by Luke. This, as we have been saying, is no chance order; it goes to the centre of the Christian faith. The Word became flesh before the flesh became word. Jesus talked what He lived and He lived what He talked.

With all other teachers it is the opposite. 'Follow the truth I bring to you, not me,' they all say. Jesus says: 'Follow Me and you will know the truth.' The truth He shared was operative in His own life. That is why the truth came across with such authority – deep answered to deep. In Christ we have the feel of consistency – His words and deeds hold together for they are two sides of the one reality. We follow Jesus' example – our doing and our teaching must be one. If there is no 'doing' then our teaching will be just empty words.

FURTHER STUDY

Acts 18:1-4;
2 Thess. 3:6-15;
2 Tim. 3:1-17

1. How was Paul's life consistent?

2. What equips us for good work?

A Sikh driver for a missionary in India said to the missionary: 'Sahib, let me preach one night to these people.' 'What would you preach about?' asked the missionary. 'I would preach against liquor and tobacco,' he said. 'But,' responded the missionary, 'you use both.' 'Yes I do,' the Sikh replied, 'but these people don't know that.' Eventually they would have discovered that for, as our text tells us, there is nothing covered that will not be revealed. People sense reality as they sense beauty and harmony. When Jesus spoke, reality spoke. One preacher says of Him: 'When Jesus spoke, people knew that His teaching was not the exposition of a text but the exposure of the texture of His being.' Our doing and our teaching must be one, or we do not teach.

O God, give me a desire, I pray, to be as good on the inside as I may appear on the outside. Grant that my words and my deeds may speak one message - Your message. In Jesus' name. Amen.

'At home in His love'

'If you obey my commands, you will remain in my love' (v10)

Another of Jesus' legacies is His commands. Jesus Himself obeyed His Father's commands. Although Jesus was secure in His Father's unqualified love and approval, He did not just bask in that love in an indulgent way, oblivious to the responsibilities love enjoins. By keeping His Father's commands, Jesus remained in His love: how snug and secure He was in it. Eugene Peterson's paraphrase *The Message* uses the expression 'at home in his love'.

This loving eagerness to do the Father's will is a model for us all. Even the Son of God learned the true cost of such love by what He was called upon to endure, demonstrated by trust. But the mutual love of Father and Son sustained Jesus' sense of purpose. After all, love is *proved* by obedience, is it not? It isn't that our obedience earns God's love as if, in Don Carson's words, 'His love is so sullen and miserly that it has to be wrenched from Him by a kind of moral bribery'. No, love for Christ overflows in wanting to do His will. Neither is it some grim, grudging, dutiful allegiance. It is clear Jesus found supreme joy in this love relationship of obedience to the Father. And we, likewise, can find delight in doing Christ's will and walking in His way.

FURTHER STUDY

Psa. 40:6-8;
Heb. 5:1-10,
10:5-7

1. What did obedience mean for Christ?

2. What was Christ's desire?

The deepest form of joy is not dependent on passing moods or events but springs from trust in and dependence on Jesus Christ. You can be sure of this: no more confused Christian exists than the one who is short-changing God over the matter of trust and obedience. When you draw generously on His love and obey His commands then it follows, as night follows day, that you will drink deeply from the well of His lasting joy.

My Father and my God, just as Your love was revealed in the Word made flesh so may the word of love be made flesh in me and be evident to all I shall meet this day. In Jesus' name. Amen.

Love – a command?

FOR READING & MEDITATION - JOHN 15:12-17

'My command is this: Love each other as I have loved you.' (v12)

Of all the commands that Jesus left as His legacy to us none is more challenging than this: 'Love each other as I have loved you.' His love is the standard and the source of our love for each other. But how can anyone be *commanded* to love? Some psychologists would say that it is impossible by an act of will to generate love. When we follow Jesus, His love so fills our hearts that we need to receive from God and then decide by an act of will to let that love flow out to others. We do not manufacture it, we simply decide to let it flow out in the same measure that it flows in.

Tragically, many parts of the Christian Church get involved in a civil war. Some believers put more energy into wrestling with each other than with the spiritual forces of evil. Nothing more quickly brings the gospel into disrepute. Once again I urge you to consider how different the Church would be if everyone who found himself or herself in disagreement with another Christian followed Jesus' command to love as He loves. I believe that Christians cannot excuse themselves by saying: 'I do not feel love in my heart.' The love of Jesus is there and we need to release that love. Every Christian has a reservoir of love deposited within them by the Saviour.

FURTHER STUDY

Rom. 5:1-5; Gal. 2:11-14

1. What has God done?

2. Contrast Peter's and Paul's love for others.

Paul, who was without doubt one of the greatest of Christians, said: 'Christ's love compels us' (2 Cor. 5:14). In other words, he was motivated by the love of Christ. This cuts deep. To be motivated by the love of Christ means that we draw on His love and do the loving thing – we love both in word and in deed. If we say it's impossible we are simply saying that though Christ's love is in our hearts it doesn't motivate us.

Father, You have commanded me to love. Please help me now to obey. I have been chosen to bear fruit, especially the fruit of loving others. I offer no excuses. From today I will love as I am loved. In Jesus' name. Amen.

The new commandment

FOR READING & MEDITATION - JOHN 13:31-38

'A new command I give you: Love one another. As I have loved you, so you must love one another.' (v34)

The command to love was not new because it had never been issued before but because it had never been *seen* before. It was new because it was measured by an unprecedented love – Jesus' love for His disciples. Nothing in them gave rise to it and nothing in them could extinguish it.

Some scholars suggest that the farewell passages in John are the New Testament equivalent of the book of Deuteronomy in which Moses bids farewell to the generation on the verge of entering the Promised Land. Certainly the same themes occur, namely of knowing God and loving God and keeping His commandments. If this is the background to these marvellous discourses then we learn something very significant about Jesus. Not only was He putting Himself in the place of Moses as the mediator of God's covenant blessings and responsibilities, He was putting Himself in the place of God by issuing further and new commandments to the people of God. The command He issues here might be called the 'eleventh commandment'. Against the dark backdrop of the betrayal of Judas the love of Jesus shines out even more brightly. Judas misread the heart of Jesus tragically. It is not in the self-love that seeks to preserve its life but in the love which lays down its life that God is glorified. Not the love of power but the power of love will be the distinguishing mark of the new people of God.

FURTHER STUDY

Jer. 31:3-6;
1 John 4:7-21

1. What is the nature of God's love?

2. How does God live in us?

There ought to be no doubt in our minds that if we embraced this legacy of love and followed Jesus' command to love one another then the people of the world would have no doubt in their minds that we are truly Christ's disciples.

God, how I long that my love shall be like Your love – a love that can't help but love. Work in me to release the love You have placed there so that my love will be as extravagant and indiscriminate as Yours – in my small way. Amen.

'We will still love you'

FOR READING & MEDITATION – MATTHEW 5:38-48
'But I tell you, Do not resist an evil person.' (v39)

Jesus' command to 'Love your enemies' (v44) is not only challenging but revolutionary. For first-century Jews the obvious enemy was the Roman occupying power with its humiliating demands. Yet Jesus said: 'If someone forces you to go one mile, go with him two miles' (v41).

Christian love, as Martin Luther King put it, is the most durable quality in the world. Defiantly, at the height of the Civil Rights crisis, he wrote from a Georgia prison: 'Do to us what you will and we will still love you ... Send your hooded perpetrators of violence into our community at the midnight hour and beat us and leave us half dead, and we will still love you ... One day we shall win freedom, but not only for ourselves. We shall so appeal to your hearts and conscience that we shall win *you* in the process, and our victory will be a double victory.'

Of course, we may not face such exceptional opposition as he did. Our 'enemies' may be more mundane: someone who gratuitously insults us, someone who strikes us on our right cheek (v39), someone who sues us unjustly (v40), or someone who borrows from us irresponsibly (v42). By our reactions to all such people we show that love is not a medium of exchange – we do not expect to get back what we give. Rather, we risk a loving gesture and action, trusting to get our reward from God alone (v46). In the end our biggest challenge may be to love an 'enemy' by greeting them in the street (v47)!

There are two ways to get rid of a block of ice: either smash it with a hammer or melt it. What you cannot get around, melt with love. And in the event it doesn't melt then still go on loving, for the loving are the inevitable winners in any situation.

FURTHER STUDY

1 Cor. 13:1-13;
1 John 3:10-18

1. Why may spiritual people be useless?

2. How do we know what love is like?

O Jesus, teach me to be a more loving person. Help me to melt every situation by Your love. Help me understand that I cannot fail if I love, even if my love fails to accomplish its ends, for the more I love the more loving I become. Amen.

'The full treatment'

FOR READING & MEDITATION - MATTHEW 5:43-48

'Be perfect, therefore, as your heavenly Father is perfect.' (v48)

Today's command, given in today's text, may once again sound like an impossible ideal. It is helpful to note that the word 'perfect' (*teleios* in the Greek) is best translated as 'complete' or 'mature' – a reference not so much to God's moral perfection as to His generosity of heart. If God's sun shines and His rain falls equally on the just and the unjust in indiscriminate goodness then to go on loving people who mistreat us is to develop what theologian Dale Bruner calls the 'poise of maturity'. Jesus' command is a challenge not to settle for anything less than what the Father wants to give us and wants to do with our lives.

FURTHER STUDY

Eph. 3:14-21; 4:11-16

1. How can we experience the fullness of God?

2. How can we experience the fullness of Christ?

When CWR bought Waverley Abbey House it was disused and derelict. The aim then was not merely to tidy up a small corner here or add a conservatory there but to renovate the whole building, transforming it into the beautiful, though in many ways still unfinished, place it is today. Similarly, the Father is the 'Great Redeveloper' of our lives. He is not content merely to add a bit of religion to a corner of our lives. He is committed to our total renovation. In Christ we embark on a lifetime reconstruction programme. To be perfect as God is perfect is to be willing, as Eugene Peterson puts it, to 'live out your God-given identity'. Thankfully, our heavenly Father is graciously and patiently still working on us to complete that task to His satisfaction.

And don't forget that 'Love never fails' (1 Cor. 13:8). It always finds ways of expressing itself, and in doing so it makes the person who loves more loving. As we said yesterday, even if you see no results of your loving you still become more loving for having loved. There is nothing higher.

Father, thank You for reminding me of the fact that I cannot fail if I love, even if my love fails to accomplish its ends, for in expressing love I become more loving. I grow in love. How wonderful. Amen.

Waverley
COURSES & EVENTS

ble Discovery Course:
e Clash of Kingdoms
An Exploration of the
ook of Revelation
d by Philip Greenslade

3 DAYS

er three days we will explore the
ophetic challenge of the book of
velation to the Church in our own
ne as it encourages and exhorts
e Church to be a countercultural
mmunity. We ask how disciples
n remain faithful under pressure
d look at the contrast between
 e worship and idolatrous
rship. Together we will reflect
the resounding victory of love
vealed through the cross.

nue: Pilgrim Hall
es-Thurs 6-8 May
20 Residential/£165 Non-residential

Bible Discovery Weekend:
Strength Made Perfect
in Weakness
Led by Philip Greenslade

3 DAYS

This weekend will reflect on Paul's
vision of the cruciform life as spelled
out in his Second Letter to the
Corinthians. Enter once again into
the mystery of your baptism as we
explore the remarkably paradoxical
nature of living in union with Christ:
dying to live, defeated to conquer,
poverty and riches, strength through
weakness. Discover again the drama
of discipleship as experienced and
commended by the Apostle Paul as
the dynamic new covenant living to
be enjoyed by every Christian.

Venue: Waverley Abbey House
Fri-Sun 20-22 June
£220 Residential/£165 Non-residential
Early Bird Price (Up to 28 Mar 2014)
£198 Residential/
£148.50 Non-residential

or further info/To book: **www.cwr.org.uk** or call **+44 (0)1252 784719**.
Prices and dates correct at the time of printing.

Introduction to Biblical Care and Counselling
Led by Angie Coombes, Richard Laws and team

5 DAYS

This five day foundation course is an ideal way to begin learning how to put your desire to help people into effective practice. You will be encouraged to reflect on your own life in the light of the biblical model presente before using the principles to help others. Our approach has transformed the lives of so many who have been on this course. Key features include; the biblica basis for pastoral care and counselling, how to deal with life's basic issues successfully and essential facts every people-helper should know.

Venue: Waverley Abbey House
Mon–Fri 17–21 March, Mon–Fri 9–13 June, Mon–Fri 17–21 November
Venue: Pilgrim Hall
Mon–Fri 11–15 August
£450 Residential/£340 non-residential

'I found the course extremely comprehensive and it was run with great sensitivity and professionalism.'

For further info/To book: **www.cwr.org.uk** or call **+44 (0)1252 784719**.
Prices and dates correct at the time of printing.

Developing an Integrative Christian Approach to Counselling

4 DAYS

Led by Mary Higginson

Are you a trained counsellor wanting to integrate your Christian world-view into your professional work? This introductory course will provide an overview and basic working understanding of the Waverley Integrative Framework and three-phase approach to counselling, and include the opportunity for discussion of case studies. It will demonstrate how elements from cognitive, psychodynamic and person-centred approaches can be included within the Waverley Integrative Framework, and will encourage participants to consider ways of working with both Christian and non-Christian clients. There will be plenty of opportunity for discussion, especially of spirituality, and for personal reflection on the material. The course also offers 25 hours of CPD for all participants.

Venue: Waverley Abbey House
Wed-Sat 27-30 August
£495 Residential/£412.50 Non-residential
Early Bird Prices £445.50 Residential/
£371.25 Non-residential
(up to 4 Jun 2014)

'I feel nurtured and heard - also inspired and challenged to go deeper.'

The Bible in a Day
Led by Andy Peck

How can we read, interpret and personally apply the Bible today? This broad overview of the Bible's content, themes and priorities emphasises the centrality of Christ as the heart of God's revelation and will inspire you to go on discovering the riches of Scripture for the rest of your life.

Venue: Waverley Abbey House
Thursday 8 May
£38.50 including lunch
Early Bird Price £34.65
(up to 13 Mar 2014)

The Life and Times of Jesus
Led by Andy Peck

Learn how to serve Jesus today and share His message more effectively by considering the full story told in the Gospels: His three years in public ministry in regard to chronology, local geopgraphy and its place within the Bible's overall narrative, His key teaching and miracles and why He was killed. Pictures from Israel today will give perspective.

Venue: Waverley Abbey House
Thursday 9 October
£38.50 including lunch
Early Bird Price £34.65
(up to 14 Aug 2014)

Future Bible Discovery Weekend
Venue: Waverley Abbey House
Fri-Sun 14-16 November

'Clarified the chronology of Bible events and shown how God's purpose is seen throughout.'

We can come to you

All you need is a venue! If you would like us to bring any of our popular short courses to your local community contact us at the details below.

FOR WOMEN

Being a Secure Woman - in an Insecure World*
Women Mentoring Women
Seasons
Designed for Living**

SEMINARS FOR EVERYONE

Faith, Hope, Love and Everything in Between
7 Laws for Life
Christ Empowered Living
Understanding Yourself, Understanding Others
Coaching and Mentoring Others
The Bible in a Day
Insight Days - topics such as depression, anger, self-esteem, anxiety
Refreshing Your Spiritual Life
Vital Tools for a Small Group Leader

*Formerly 'How to be a Secure Woman'
**Formerly 'Designer Living'

For full details (including costs) and to arrange a seminar in your area, please call **+44 (0)1252 784719** or email **training@cwr.org.uk**

Women's Weekends

Women's weekends offer time and space to enjoy the company of God and others, to listen, laugh and share, to reflect creatively and pray in beautiful surroundings.

Reaching for Jesus' Hand

Led by Paula Buchel and Karen Case-Green

WEEKEND

In Matthew's gospel we read the story of Peter walking out on the water in response to Jesus' call. But when he sees the waves at his feet and the impossibility of what he's ventured into, he begins to sink. Wonderfully, this isn't the end of the story – we are told that Jesus reached out His hand to Peter and caught him. Sometimes we feel that the sea of life is raging around us. But in the midst of all our challenges He is there, calling us to come to Him, and reaching out to grasp us with a firm and steady hand. At this time, the beginning of spring, come and be encouraged by this truth and draw closer to Him.

Venue: Waverley Abbey House
Fri-Sun 28-30 March
£195 Residential/£140 Non-residential (includes lunches/evening meals)

Knowing True Joy

Led by Paula Buchel and the Women's ministry team

WEEKEND

Paul wrote the book of Philippians while he was in very difficult circumstances (in prison) and yet his writing seems to overflow with joy. In it he exhorts us to rejoice in the Lord always, whatever our circumstances and He promises us that His peace will guard both our hearts and our minds. Come and be refreshed, draw closer to God and explore what it means to rejoice in Him always.

Venue: Pilgrim Hall
Fri-Sun 6-8 June
Residential:
£178 (single non-ensuite);
£195 (shared ensuite)
Early Bird Prices £160/£176 (up to 14 Mar)
Non-residential:
£140 (includes lunches/evening meals)
Early Bird Price £126 (up to 14 Mar)

For further info/To book: **www.cwr.org.uk** or call **+44 (0)1252 784719**. Prices and dates correct at the time of printing.

Counselling Training Enquirers' Event

Are you wondering if counselling training is for you? Would you like to know more about any of the courses mentioned here? If so, you are warmly invited to one of our Enquirers' Days, where you can meet the tutors, sit in on a counselling lecture and ask questions.

Venue: Waverley Abbey House
Saturday 26 April (10am – 1pm)
Saturday 1 November (10am – 1pm)

Venue: Pilgrim Hall
Friday 20 June (12pm – 3pm)

These events are FREE

'Very helpful day which confirmed the path I should take.'

Preparation for Marriage

Led by Mick & Lynette Brooks with Lynn & Andrew Penson

Build a firm Biblical foundation as you consider the nature of Christian marriage, love and sexuality. With help from the Myers-Briggs Type Indicator®, develop mutual understanding and learn to handle conflict and avoid marriage breakdown, as you identify the strengths, weaknesses and potential stress points in your relationship.

Venue: Waverley Abbey House
Fri–Sun 7–9 March
£390 residential per couple
(£195 per person if being paid for separately)

'Awesome! It's been great to be taught by people who have really lived it, who speak from the heart and know what they're talking about!'

Marriage on Track

Led by Lynn & Andrew Penson

Enjoy a weekend together in beautiful surroundings offering the opportunity to consider what Christian marriage means and explore topics such as communication, handling conflict, sexual intimacy, expressing love and understanding your partner with the help of the Myers-Briggs Type Indicator®. Celebrate your marriage with a romantic dinner à deux on Saturday evening!

Venue: Waverley Abbey House
Fri–Sun 13–15 June
£390 residential per couple
Early Bird Price £351 (up to 21 Mar 2014)

Holiness - a force that changes

FOR READING & MEDITATION - LUKE 6:27-36

'Be merciful, just as your Father is merciful.' (v36)

We continue to reflect on Jesus' astonishing command, delivered in His Sermon on the Mount: 'Be perfect, therefore, as your heavenly Father is perfect' (Matt. 5:48). In Luke's version, which is often called the 'Sermon on the Plain', the same thought is given, but the variation in wording is significant and confirms the interpretation we took yesterday: 'Be merciful, just as your Father is merciful.'

When Jesus first said these words they must have been regarded as very provocative. Israel's national charter, repeated often in the book of Leviticus, was to 'Be holy because I, the LORD your God, am holy' (Lev. 19:2). Israel was to be a distinctive people displaying God's character in the world. But in the time of Jesus some strict religious groups, such as the Pharisees and teachers of the law, interpreted this calling in an inward and exclusive sense. They drew tighter and tighter boundaries, excluding more and more people as 'sinners' and therefore outside the circle of God's covenant love. Not for one moment does Jesus deny the call to be holy. But He shows that God's holiness is not merely a standard that condemns sinners but an outgoing force that changes sinners. For Jesus, to be holy does not mean to withdraw self-righteously from the contagion of sinners but to reach out and embrace sinners with a cleansing wave of healing compassion. We are saved by a holiness that condemns our sin but also yearns and arranges for our salvation, if indeed we desire it. Even God cannot save us if we do not want to be saved.

Consider this as you go out into the day: the command to be holy as God is holy is best fulfilled by being merciful as your heavenly Father is merciful.

FURTHER STUDY

Psa. 86:1-17; Matt. 12:1-14

1. Describe God's character.

2. What did holiness mean to Jesus?

O Father, make me more like You I pray. Thank You for showing me that being holy does not involve withdrawing from sinners lest they stain my soul but rather going into the midst of them to seek and to save. Amen.

A simple remedy

FOR READING & MEDITATION - MATTHEW 6:25-34

'But seek first his kingdom and his righteousness, and all these things will be given to you as well.' (v33)

It is understandable that in seeking answers to the everyday anxieties that overshadow our lives and to the decisions we have to make we sometimes grow confused. The multiplicity of choices available to us can paralyse us. In a sincere attempt to please God we can tie ourselves into knots trying to find guidance. Today's command from Jesus cuts like a sharp knife through many of the knots created by our perplexities concerning guidance and dispels much of the confusion that exists about this subject.

FURTHER STUDY

Matt. 6:19-24;
Luke 10:38-42

1. What may distract us from God's kingdom?

2. How may the work of God distract us from God?

After theologian Gerald Sittser lost his wife, mother, and four-year-old daughter in a drunk-driving accident he wrote one of the most moving and helpful books on bereavement ever written. He called that book *A Grace Disguised*. More recently he has written a book entitled *The Will of God as a Way of Life* in which he reflects on the experience and seeks to come to terms with it. In it he points out that we already know the will of God: it is contained in today's command. Amid so many choices, he writes: 'We may wish that God would tell us exactly what to do, where to go, and how to choose. Yet Jesus only requires that we make sure our heart is good, our motives are pure, and our basic direction is right, pointing toward the "true north" of the kingdom of God.' Gerald Sittser goes on to say, rightly so, that: 'We can, in good conscience, choose from among any number of reasonable alternatives and continue to do the will of God. In the end what matters is that we seek God's kingdom and righteousness.'

It might sound simplistic to say but it is true nevertheless: put God and His glory first and foremost in everything and you will have few difficulties with divine guidance.

Father, I am so thankful that You have a simple remedy for everything – simple but not simplistic. Help me to take it. In Jesus' name. Amen.

Why we are instructed to go

FOR READING & MEDITATION - MATTHEW 28:16-20

'... go and make disciples of all nations, baptising them in the name of the Father ... Son and ... Holy Spirit' (v19)

The words before us today are sometimes referred to as 'the missionary mandate'. At first glance this command appears terribly intimidating for it presents an overwhelming and awesome task. But, in truth, it serves to tell us more about Jesus and His greatness than it does about ourselves and our inability. We should keep that in mind as we focus on these amazing instructions.

This command of Jesus says nothing about our capacity to take control of the world and everything about His authority over the world. The emphasis is not so much on going but making: 'go and *make* disciples'. This single imperative ('make disciples of all nations') is supported by three participles (going ... baptising ... teaching) that explain how this is to be done. Of course, 'going' is necessary. But when we embark on mission we must always remember that we go, not to make Jesus Lord, because He already is Lord. The aim of mission is not to encourage people to make decisions but to become disciples – in other words, the enabling of others to live lives worthy of God. Disciples are made by immersing them through baptism into the full-scale Trinity-life and love of God. And they continue to be made by ongoing instruction in everything Jesus said and taught.

FURTHER STUDY

Acts 2:42-47, 4:32-35; Rom. 10:8-15

1. How did the early believers obey Jesus' command?

2. Why is it imperative 'to go'?

These are the 'standing orders' of the Church. For Christ's people, worshipful but still doubtful, what matters most is the majesty of the master, not the magnitude of the task. The 'all' found in these verses speaks volumes: *all* authority, in *all* nations, *all* Jesus' commands, for *all* time. And remember, too, that what our divine commander asks us to go and do for the world is less than He has already done for the world.

Father, help us as Your disciples to make more disciples, and may our own lives exhibit true discipleship, for we can take people no further than we have gone ourselves. In Jesus' name. Amen.

My joy - your joy

FOR READING & MEDITATION - JOHN 15:1-17

'I have told you this so that my joy may be in you and that your joy may be complete.' (v11)

The legacy of Jesus which we will consider now is joy. What a valuable, even priceless commodity this is. It is no accident that our Lord talks about joy in the context of love, for joy is a by-product of love. Thomas Aquinas said: 'No one truly has joy unless he lives in love.' If we seek joy first it will elude us, but when we allow God's love to abound in our hearts then we don't have to seek joy; it will seek us. It is doubtless true to say that no human being on this planet has experienced joy as Jesus did. His heart, unsullied, was able to taste the joy of unclouded communion with God His Father, and that is the joy He wanted to impart to His disciples.

FURTHER STUDY

Neh. 8:8-12;
Psa. 16:1-11

1. What gave the people strength and encouragement?

2. What is associated with intimacy with God?

There is something interesting in today's text. Jesus talks about 'my joy' and 'your joy', and says that when *His* joy is in us then *our* joy is complete. Eugene Peterson paraphrases it thus: 'I've told you these things for a purpose: that my joy might be your joy, and your joy wholly mature.' Our joy, it seems, can never rise to the pinnacle of its potential until Jesus' joy enters into us. As we receive His joy, ours is made complete. That is why we can say without fear of successful contradiction that people who do not know God can never know joy in the way they were intended to.

Let there be no mistake about it: we were designed in the beginning for unimagined joy. But sin has damaged our souls, and the joy we experience in the world around is nothing compared to the joy our souls experience when Christ's joy enters into ours. 'Joy,' said Wendell Harris, a writer from a past generation, 'is the strength of the people of God.' It is. And it comes not from our strength but from His strength being added to ours.

O Father, help me take my birthright of joy and live the life for which I was made. You designed me for something more joyful than the world around can give me. I want joy to enter into me and me into it. In Jesus' name. Amen.

Jumping for joy

FOR READING & MEDITATION - LUKE 10:1-24

'At that time Jesus, full of joy through the Holy Spirit, said,
"I praise you, Father"' (v21)

There are some who say they find it difficult to associate Jesus with joy. Their argument goes like this: everywhere in the Gospels we see Jesus moving forward towards the ordeal of the cross. In one place in the King James Bible He is said to carry His destination on His face (Luke 9:53). Jesus was a serious and sober man, and though He had peace like a river flowing into His soul, inwardly He was always wrestling with the prospect of His impending death – the ignominious death of the cross. Soberness rather than joy (they say) must have been the thing that characterised Him most.

Those who take this view should look a little more closely at the passage before us today. When His disciples came back from their mission with reports of their ministry and service, Jesus gave thanks to the Father and, says Luke, was 'full of joy through the Holy Spirit'. The Greek words translated here as 'full of joy', says Paul Thigpen, author of *Blood of the Martyrs, Seed of the Church*, literally mean 'jumping for joy'. It might be difficult for some to imagine, but if this is so then Jesus would have been jumping for joy over the fact that people had been delivered from Satan's power.

What a scene for the disciples to behold: the Son, in the Spirit, praising the Father and exploding with joy. Did He dance, leap around, and jump up and down with delight? It's possible. 'For a moment,' says Paul Thigpen, 'the veil of heaven was pulled back and a handful of humble souls caught a glimpse of the divine delight that flows for ever within the blessed Trinity.' Such a vision would make anyone jump for joy.

FURTHER STUDY

Luke 15:1-10;
Heb. 12:1-3

1. What happens when someone becomes a Christian?

2. Why did Jesus endure the cross?

Lord Jesus Christ, I've never imagined You jumping for joy. But I see how such a vision as You saw would thrill Your soul with delight. I open my heart for that same vision to delight my soul. May I, too, have cause to jump for joy. Amen.

Opportunities to train in
Counselling and people-helping

For those with a heart to help others, CWR offers Counselling training from a Christian worldview.

HOW DO I FIND OUT?

Come to one of our **Counselling Training Enquirers' Days**. These are free events when you can meet tutors, ask questions and sit in on a counselling lecture
Sat 26 April
Venue: Waverley Abbey House

'a very helpful day which confirmed the path I should take.'

HOW CAN I BEGIN?

Introduction to Biblical Care and Counselling is a five-day foundation course; an ideal starting point for reflection on your own life in the light of the biblical model, before using these principles to help others.
Key features include:

· the biblical basis for pastoral care and counselling
· essential facts that every people-helper should know
· developing and sharpening counselling skills
· how to successfully deal with life's basic issues
· a step-by-step personal strategy for pastoral care and counselling.

Mon–Fri 17-21 March
Led by Angie Coombes and Team
Venue: Waverley Abbey House

'A great course, equipping us to come alongside others in their time of need.'

WHAT NEXT?

CWR provides a number of options for accredited study, offered in a variety of flexible learning packages:

- **Certificate of Christian Counselling (ACC level 3)** is a one-year course offered over one week and nine weekends. This also forms Year 1 of our BA course.
- **BA (Hons) Counselling** is validated by the University of Roehampton and led by our CWR team of lecturers and highly experienced counselling practitioners. This flexible programme offers the opportunity to study for a Dip HE in 3 years, or BA (Hons) over 4–5 years.
- **MA Counselling,** also validated by Roehampton, is offered in two formats. One is a graduate entry programme enabling you to also train as a counsellor. The alternative MA in Relational Counselling and Psychotherapy is for experienced counsellors.

To find out more about our wide-ranging counselling training programme, conducted at our two training centres, Waverley Abbey House in Surrey and Pilgrim Hall in East Sussex, please visit **www.cwr.org.uk/training** or contact Waverley Courses and Events at training@cwr.org.uk, tel. +44 (0)1252 784719.

'Come to the party'

FOR READING & MEDITATION - MATTHEW 22:1-14

'The kingdom of heaven is like a king who prepared a wedding banquet for his son.' (v2)

We saw yesterday how Jesus was filled with joy when His disciples came back from their mission. Jesus is not content simply to enjoy the fellowship of the Father and participate in 'the divine delight that flows for ever within the blessed Trinity'; He longs for us also to enter into His joy.

In the parable we have read today Jesus tells us that the kingdom of God is like a wedding feast. The invitation has gone out: 'Come to the party. Rejoice with the king whose son has found a beloved bride.' The parable, of course, is filled with irony. The first ones invited to join the celebration actually refused it. Some insisted they were much too busy to rejoice; others appeared to despise those who were foolish enough (in their eyes) to make merry. Who dares to celebrate when life is so full of difficulties? Those who see with the eye of faith. Only these can look beyond the present darkness to see, as one preacher has put it, that: 'In the beginning was Joy, and the Joy was within God, and the Joy flowed from God.' If only we knew the joy that pulses in the midst of the Trinity then we might have a whole new approach to the Christian life.

FURTHER STUDY

Zeph. 3:14-20;
Luke 7:29-35

1. What causes us to rejoice?

2. Why did religious people criticise Jesus?

In Zephaniah we find a startling image. The prophet pictures God as a mighty warrior who exults in His victory over sin and the sinners He reclaims. God, says Zephaniah, 'will take great delight in you … he will rejoice over you with singing' (Zeph. 3:17). The word translated 'delight' means 'unbridled gladness', and the phrase 'with singing' means to 'spin around with tumultuous joy'. Whoever has seen Jesus has seen the Father, so we should not be surprised to see this joyful picture of God made flesh in the life of our Lord.

My Father and my God, how can I ever thank You enough that the joy that characterises the Trinity has, through what Your Son did for me on Calvary, been set in my heart too? Blessed be Your name for ever. Amen.

FOR READING & MEDITATION - ISAIAH 35:1-10
'... the ransomed of the LORD will return. They will enter Zion with singing; everlasting joy will crown their heads.' (v10)

'Jesus Christ,' said Oswald Chambers, 'does not come to a man and say, "Cheer up". He plants within a man the miracle of the joy of God's own nature.' What a legacy. How sad that among the many misunderstandings which people have concerning the Christian faith is the idea that to receive Jesus Christ into one's life is to be made miserable. The fact that there is a cross at the heart of our faith, and that following Christ involves self-discipline, does not alter this central truth: to know Jesus is to know joy.

Dr W.E. Sangster said: 'The Greek word generally used for joy in the New Testament is *chara* – a strong and powerful word indicating hilariousness.' He continued: 'Joy is not resignation wearing a wan smile. It is exuberant and, on occasion, boisterous.' People too much imprisoned in the proprieties and still with good manners have even thought in their inhibited way that there is a touch of the vulgar in Christian joy. How sad. How very sad. The founder of Christianity has bequeathed to us a faith which is the most joyous, the least repressive, the least forbidding of all the religions found on earth.

FURTHER STUDY

Psa. 149:1-5; Isa. 12:1-6

1. How can dancing be a form of praise?

2. What is a source of joy?

Dr L.P. Jacks, author of *The Lost Radiance of the Christian Religion*, says: 'There is no faith which throws off the burden of life so completely, which escapes so swiftly from our moods, which gives so large a scope for the high spirits of the soul as the faith which Jesus Christ gives. Christianity does not brood upon the sorrows of mankind. It recognises them but does not dwell on them. It is always music that you hear and sometimes dancing as well.' *Always music that you hear.* Those who do not hear cannot be listening.

Gracious and loving Father, may my ear ever be open to the music which Your gospel makes available to me. Tune my whole being to the wavelength of the Trinity. In Jesus' name. Amen.

Pleasure versus joy

FOR READING & MEDITATION - ROMANS 15:1-13

'May the God of hope fill you with all joy and peace as you trust in him' (v13)

It's all too easy to mistake pleasure for joy, so today we explore the ways in which they differ. Everyone experiences pleasure. Indeed, if we were to listen to them we would be led to believe that only they know what pleasure is. However, the slightest probing beneath the surface reveals the great difference between pleasure and joy.

Pleasure often depends on circumstances. It demands that the conditions of life be healthy, or at least kindly, and it can be stolen quite easily by a simple thing such as a headache. Joy, the deep-seated peace that Jesus gives, is independent of health or circumstances. It still bubbles up in Christians even when strength and health and friends are gone – when circumstances are not just unkind but desperate. Again, pleasures satiate and do not satisfy. It is easy to have too much pleasure, and when the point of satiety is passed loathing sets in. The thing for which the heart craved it no longer craves. Joy, on the other hand, never satiates. The Christian says: 'I have enough but not too much to long for more.'

Pleasure tends to always remains superficial; also it continues to exist by ignoring the difficulties and unanswered problems of life. It is like the merriment of Christmas in a home where Christ is not believed in – a party without purpose. There may be fun and frolics but underneath there is an empty aching heart.

Joy, supernatural joy, is so different. It bubbles up from deep inner contentment. It may flame into rapture, burst out in song, even express itself in dance or sink into peace, but whatever form it takes it possesses the whole personality. Joy is bliss, sheer unadulterated bliss. And it comes only from Jesus.

FURTHER STUDY

Isa. 60:13-17;
Heb. 11:24-28;
James 1:2-3,12

1. Contrast the longevity of joy and pleasure.

2. Why can we rejoice in difficult times?

Father, I am so thankful that Your Son's joy is now my joy – a joy that can stand anything. I am glad, too, that it is a joy that not only lasts but gets richer and fuller all the time. Amen.

Joy-snatchers

FOR READING & MEDITATION - JOHN 16:17-33

'... Now is your time of grief, but I will see you again and you will
rejoice, and no-one will take away your joy.' (v22)

What tremendous encouragement this verse breathes
into our souls: ultimately, no one can take away our
joy. The joy that Jesus gives is ours for ever. There are, of
course, many things that would try to snatch it away, such
as anxiety and fear, comparing and coveting, sin, busyness
and over-commitment.

One theologian, however, argues that the opposite of joy
is not sorrow but unbelief. He may well be right – it may be
that what really deprives us of joy is unbelief. Even when
outward circumstances cause us sorrow, our joy can be
sustained by our belief in God and remembrance
of God's goodness in the past.

The apostle Paul tells us in 2 Corinthians that he
was 'sorrowful, yet always rejoicing' (2 Cor. 6:10).
Paul experienced a great deal of sorrow, so if it is
sorrow that takes away joy then Paul would be the
most joyless person in the New Testament. Yet he
wrote: 'I am greatly encouraged; in all our troubles
my joy knows no bounds' (2 Cor. 7:4). When we
put our faith in what Jesus says then we take the
most significant step towards maintaining our
spiritual joy. Trust and faith demolish the lies
put in our minds by Satan and allow joy to breathe freely.
The psalmist wrote this about the Lord: 'In him our hearts
rejoice, for we trust in his holy name' (Psa. 33:21).

A letter that came to us at CWR from a young man whose
father had died said this: 'When my dad fell asleep on my
mother's shoulder, never to wake on this earth again, his
face was radiant with joy. I said to my mother, repeating
the words of John 16:22: "No one will take away your joy"
[the joy of his father].' That is true of all who die in Christ;
His joy remains with them to the end.

FURTHER STUDY

Rom. 14:16-18;
1 Pet. 1:3-9

1. What
characterises
God's kingdom?

2. Why does
grief not snatch
our joy?

**Father, I am truly grateful that You have promised Your joy will
remain with me in all circumstances. No one can take it away.
Blessed be Your name for ever. Amen.**

Our heavenly Advocate

FOR READING & MEDITATION - JOHN 14:15-24

'And I will ask the Father, and he will give you another Counsellor to be with you for ever' (v16)

Another legacy which Jesus left for us is His gift of the Holy Spirit. The word Jesus uses to describe the Holy Spirit in the Greek is *parakletos*, which, as you may be aware, means 'the one called alongside to help'. How is this word best translated?

'Comforter' is misleading, except in the old English sense of 'giving strength to'. A cameo in the Bayeux tapestry shows King Harold 'comforting' his troops by prodding them into action with his lance! 'Counsellor' is better, but tends to concede too much to a culture which reduces everything to psychological terms. In fact, the word *parakletos*, or 'paraclete', almost certainly retains its legal connotation, and is best translated as 'advocate' in a legal sense. This meaning fits well with the overall picture John paints in his Gospel of Jesus – and the disciples – on trial for the truth before a hostile world. The Holy Spirit is another 'advocate' like Jesus. He will stand by the disciples just as Jesus has done. He will minister to them in self-giving love just as Jesus has done. He will challenge them and confront them when they need it just as Jesus has done.

FURTHER STUDY

Luke 12:11-12;
21:10-19;
John 7:37-39

1. What legacy does Jesus promise?

2. What is a consequence of Jesus' glorification?

Many think the Holy Spirit's role is solely to provide us with comfort. However, He accomplishes far more than that. We should always remember that the Holy Spirit is with us to defend and prompt and support us. This will be a great reassurance to those who are undergoing severe trials in relation to their commitment to Christ. A world built on lies, deceit and unreality is a stranger to the Spirit of truth. But the Spirit comes alongside us to enable us to speak and live the truth, helping us to follow Jesus who is the Truth.

O Father, how comforting it is to know that the Holy Spirit is my advocate. I stretch out both hands to take all the strength I need from Him to face the day. But help me not only to take but to give also. In Jesus' name. Amen.

Always there

FOR READING & MEDITATION - JOHN 14:25-26

'But the Counsellor, the Holy Spirit ... will teach you all things and will remind you of everything I have said to you.' (v26)

We continue reflecting on the wonderful legacy Jesus left when He bequeathed to us the crowning gift of the Holy Spirit. We might well imagine that Jesus' first request when arriving in glory after His ascension was: 'Father, the channel between earth and heaven is now open – send them the Holy Spirit.'

The Holy Spirit, we said yesterday, is another advocate like Jesus. As Jesus is our advocate in heaven before the Father's throne so the Spirit is our advocate on earth in the courtroom of the world. The Holy Spirit will act only in the name of, or on the authority of, Jesus. His mission is to argue the case for the truth as it is in Jesus, and He will do this in us and through us. Everything Jesus said, which the disciples initially misunderstood, the Holy Spirit will make plain. The Holy Spirit does not bring startling unheard-of revelation – as some today suppose – but unveils the revelation that Jesus brought. There would be far less error in the Christian Church if teachers and preachers would remember that He acts as our advocate before a sceptical world, not merely by giving us peaceful feelings, but by instructing us in the truth. He is also our teacher. None of the new insights He gives, the new powers He bestows, or the new initiatives He launches will ever be detached from the Father's loving will or discredit the name of Jesus. The holy Trinity acts in concert on our behalf.

So, as you seek to be a distinctive disciple of Jesus, at home or work, in weakness or under pressure, you can be assured of the Holy Spirit's total support. He will never desert you. You can turn a deaf ear to Him but He will be at your side still.

FURTHER STUDY

1 Cor. 2:9-16;
2 Pet. 1:16-21

1. What is unique about the Holy Spirit?

2. How were the Scriptures drafted?

Father, as I contemplate where I would be today but for the Holy Spirit, my wonderful Advocate, my heart rises in gratitude and praise for His constant advocacy in my life. Thank You dear Father. Amen.

The senior partner

FOR READING & MEDITATION - JOHN 15:18-27

'When the Counsellor comes ... the Spirit of truth who goes out from the Father, he will testify about me.' (v26)

Through the prophet Isaiah, God once challenged Israel to stand up and be counted as His witnesses at the trial of the nations who were mocking God's claims to be the one Creator and Lord. Only Israel could verify this by giving her testimony (see Isa. 43:9-13). Now, as Jesus' life on earth is drawing to a close, we see a tragic reversal of the situation: it is God's own people Israel who are sceptical about the claims and identity of the One whom God has sent, so that Jesus is effectively put on trial. He looks to His disciples to testify in His defence for they have been with Him 'from the beginning' (v27) and will be able to tell the whole story.

FURTHER STUDY

Mark 12:35-37; Acts 16:6-10

1. What did Jesus explain about David's words?

2. How was the Holy Spirit Paul's senior partner?

We ourselves were not there at the beginning but we too are called to be His witnesses – to add our voices and the quality of our lives to the ongoing testimony of the wonder of Jesus. It is clear from the passage before us today that the Holy Spirit is seen as the chief witness to Jesus. When we testify to Jesus we are merely joining our voices with the voice of the Holy Spirit. The empowering comfort and advocacy of the Holy Spirit is promised to sustain us in bearing witness to the true identity of Jesus as the incarnate Son of God, the one Saviour and Lord of all.

Disciples never witness alone or unaided. How much more effective we would be in our witnessing if we remembered that a voice other than our own is speaking through every testimony we give concerning Jesus. Witnessing, then, must be seen as a partnership – we vocalise in our testimony to Jesus what the Holy Spirit passionately wants to make known. The Holy Spirit is our partner, but it must be always remembered – the *senior* partner.

O Father, what a consolation it is to know that the Holy Spirit is never passive when I am witnessing to Jesus but gloriously and wonderfully active. May I never miss an opportunity to speak up for my Lord. Amen.

Counsel for the prosecution

FOR READING & MEDITATION – JOHN 16:1-11

'When he comes, he will convict the world of guilt in regard to sin and righteousness and judgment' (v8)

In the passage we explored yesterday Jesus told the disciples that the Holy Spirit would act as the 'counsel for the defence' as they bore witness to Him. Now He tells them that the Spirit will act as 'counsel for the prosecution' in the case against the world. Acting through the disciples, the Spirit will convict the world and turn its valuation of God, Jesus and the disciples upside down. By its refusal to believe in Jesus the world's great sin will be radically exposed. Its unjust verdict passed on Jesus will be reversed, and His ascension to the Father will be His total vindication. The Spirit will also reveal that it is the world and its ruler, not Jesus, its true Lord, who was judged in the events of Easter.

What an amazing turn of events! No wonder Jesus said: 'It is for your good that I am going away' (v7). Because He returned to the Father the Spirit came, and everything looks different to Spirit-filled eyes. What an intense relief it is to realise that we are not the judge: matters of final judgment can safely be left in His hands alone. Nor, we may be pleased to learn, are we called to be the prosecuting counsel, as if we had to convince the world of the rightness of Jesus' cause. Some Christians, when witnessing, make it their goal to convince unbelievers that they should receive Christ. Our goal should be to share what we know about Jesus; it is the Holy Spirit's job to convince. We are not asked to have answers to all the questions thrown at us either, but only to do what a witness does best, which is to say what he has seen and heard.

Thanks be to God that it is the Spirit's work to convince the world of God's truth. Ours is to be faithful in bearing our testimony.

FURTHER STUDY

Acts 2:36-41; 19:1-7; 24:24-25

1. What happened when Peter and Paul preached?

2. What was the problem of the believers in Ephesus?

My Father and my God, help me to get this clear: my task is to share what I know about Jesus – it is the Holy Spirit's job to convince. May I never forget that I am a witness, not the prosecuting counsel. In Jesus' name. Amen.

Where the spotlight falls

FOR READING & MEDITATION - JOHN 16:12-15

'But when he, the Spirit of truth, comes, he will guide you into all truth.' (v13)

The Holy Spirit will not only reiterate what Jesus *has* said, stirring up our minds by way of remembrance; He will also 'guide you into all truth'. This does not mean, as some seem to think, that the Holy Spirit will teach us everything about anything – nuclear physics, for example. It means that the Spirit will lead us into all the truth we need to know about God and Jesus and our relationship with Him. In other words, it is a promise of ongoing guidance in all matters relating to being a disciple of Jesus Christ.

Through the Spirit, the disciples were told, Jesus would continue to speak and act after the ascension. Because Jesus and the Spirit are at one, we can be sure that nothing the Spirit now reveals contradicts the historic testimony to Jesus contained in the Gospels. Part of the Spirit's work is to make known 'what is yet to come' (v13), but it will be a further unfolding of the significance of what has already and majestically come to us in the Jesus who lived and died and rose again. Father, Son and Spirit share a common life and act in perfect harmony.

FURTHER STUDY

Acts 13:1-16; 4:1-12

1. How did the disciples turn the spotlight away from themselves?

2. What did they highlight?

One way to measure what purports to be the work of the Holy Spirit is to note carefully what it shows us of Jesus. The Holy Spirit does not draw attention to Himself by needless gimmicks but works wonders that glorify Jesus. He acts and behaves in ways which lead us to conclude: 'That's what Jesus does and that's the way Jesus does it.' The Holy Spirit exemplifies the divine humility in turning the spotlight away from Himself and on to Jesus. That gives us a good guideline in evaluating the things going on in some parts of the Church today that are said to be the work of the Holy Spirit.

Father, help me discern between the excesses of the flesh and the true work of the Holy Spirit. I long for true revival – one that makes Jesus more real to the world. In His Name and for His glory I pray. Amen.

The charismatic Christ

FOR READING & MEDITATION - LUKE 24:36-53

'... but stay in the city until you have been clothed with power
from on high.' (v49)

Jesus here describes the Spirit He would bestow as
coming to 'clothe with power from on high' – imagery
used in the Old Testament of Gideon (Judg. 6:34) and
Samson (Judg. 14:6) when God empowered them with the
Spirit. When Elisha succeeded Elijah he was clothed in his
master's cloak (2 Kings 2:13). The cloak was no disguise
or empty uniform but really transmitted from master to
servant the same spiritual enabling. From the time the
Spirit descended on Him at baptism, Jesus Himself was the
'charismatic Christ'. He did everything not by the inherent
powers of deity but by the imparted power of the
Spirit. So it is with His disciples. He doesn't simply
pass the baton of ministry to them; He invests
them with the same mantle of the Holy Spirit He
Himself has worn.

FURTHER STUDY

Acts 2:36-41;
Eph. 5:15-20

1. What did
Peter promise?

2. What did Paul
command?

Wonderfully, the last view the disciples had
of Jesus as He ascended was of His hands
outstretched to bless them! Blessing itself is always
associated with the Holy Spirit's anointing. Like
the Old Testament priest blessing the worshippers
(Aaron), like the head of a house blessing his family (Jacob),
like the leader blessing the nation (Moses), so Jesus blesses
His followers. The hands which had reached out to lepers
and been stretched on a cross are now uplifted in blessing.
The disciples then return with joy to praise God in the
Temple knowing that wherever their testimony for Jesus
might take them they would always be moving under the
blessing of their exalted Lord.

Like the first disciples, let us rejoice and relish the rich and
lasting legacy Jesus bestows upon His Church. His hands
are outstretched over you right now. Receive the blessing
He wants to give you – the empowerment of His Holy Spirit.

**Father, my heart is open to You. Whatever it is that You have for
me, I reach up to receive it. Fill me and empower me with Your
Holy Spirit. In Jesus' name. Amen.**

Give thanks

FOR READING & MEDITATION – LUKE 22:7-19

'And he said to them, "I have eagerly desired to eat this Passover with you before I suffer."' (v15)

As we approach Easter we consider another of Jesus' legacy gifts – the Lord's Supper. In seventeenth-century Scotland a young woman belonging to the Covenanters – a group denied their religious freedom – was on her way to a clandestine communion service when she was stopped by a soldier and asked: 'Where are you going?' 'I go to my Father's house,' she said, 'to hear read the will of His Son who has died.' Just before our Saviour died He made it clear that part of His last will and testament was a simple meal. In pondering this gift to us over the next few days we will not enter into the complex controversies that have raged around this meal nor attempt to settle any of the details. Instead we invite you to reflect devotionally and simply on this precious aspect of Christ's legacy.

FURTHER STUDY

Exod. 12:1-17;
1 Thess. 5:16-18

1. What is the origin of the annual Passover celebration?

2. What is God's will for us?

The first note to strike is that of *gratitude*. The 'thanks' Jesus uttered over the meal was more than a mere 'grace' but symbolised the offering up of His whole life as a thanksgiving offering to God. Because His self-offering was a doxology we respond by 'giving thanks'. *Eucharisteo* is the Greek word for 'to give thanks', and this is why in some churches the communion service is called the 'Eucharist'. But we remember that the emphasis is not on what we do for Him but what He has done for us. It is His sacrifice, not ours, we celebrate. Our only sacrifice is the sacrifice of praise for His!

When Holy Communion is celebrated at international gatherings it is always wonderful to observe how people who are divided by language are brought together through a common meal. Their eyes say: 'We are fellow worshippers of the one Saviour' – Jesus Christ, the Lord of all nations.

Father, my thanks will just not go into words for the gift of Your Son as my Saviour. Each time I celebrate Holy Communion may my focus be not on what I am doing for You but on what You have done for me. Amen.

'Remember Me'

FOR READING & MEDITATION - LUKE 22:17-23

'And he took bread ... and gave it to them, saying, "This is my body given for you; do this in remembrance of me."' (v19)

Jesus' instructions to His disciples for the continuance of what we call the Lord's Supper are clear and simple: *Do this in remembrance of me.* Behind this command lies Israel's long history of redemption, commemorated in the Passover feast. By keeping this feast as a memorial, Israel was to perpetuate the memory and experience afresh the impact of the original saving act of God which delivered her from Egypt. Whether Jesus and His disciples ate at, or on the eve of, Passover, the overtones of Passover are manifestly present. Jesus was doing something very radical: He was rescripting the Passover feast, placing at the centre not the first Exodus from Egypt but the new exodus from sin and death which He was about to achieve.

In this context 'remembering' is not an exercise in nostalgia, as if we are asked to screw up our minds in an attempt to imagine ourselves back in the upper room. Whenever we celebrate Holy Communion we focus, with the Holy Spirit's help, on Jesus as the one who died for us and rose again to be our ever-present Lord. We are not expected to recapture in our minds the position of the disciples in the room or just where Jesus was sitting. Pictures and paintings of this may be helpful to our imagination, but that ought not to be the central focus when we celebrate communion. We are to remember *Him* – the one who achieved for us a far greater exodus than was accomplished when the children of Israel were led out of Egypt.

In the taking, breaking, sharing, eating, and drinking, the living Christ is remembered for who He is and what He has done. This simple meal is a reminder that He who died is now gloriously alive and ever present.

FURTHER STUDY

Luke 24:13-35;
1 Cor. 11:23-26

1. When did the disciples recognise Jesus?

2. What did Paul emphasise?

Lord Jesus, help me get this right. I am to remember You not as You sat at a table in an upper room but as the One who accomplished an exodus of which I am a grateful participant. Thank You for my deliverance. Amen.

Keeping in touch

FOR READING & MEDITATION - MATTHEW 26:17-30

'... Jesus took bread ... and gave it to his disciples, saying, "Take and eat; this is my body."' (v26)

We continue to reflect on the power of the simple meal Jesus bequeathed to us which we now call Holy Communion. Some Christians tend to disparage the physical in favour of the spiritual. But precisely because of the incarnation we can hold the material and spiritual together. The touch of Jesus – skin on skin, flesh on flesh – always brought blessing to lepers and children. Jesus brought God into the realm of the material and the tangible in the very real human body He was about to offer on the cross.

Just as the physical human body of Jesus was that

FURTHER STUDY

2 Kings 23:21-25; 1 Cor. 5:7-8

1. How did Josiah get back in touch with God?

2. How is Jesus linked with Passover?

through which the eternal transcendent life of God was revealed, so a material element such as bread can be a means of opening up our imaginations for the reception of God's life to us. The phrase 'this is my body' is a powerful image which shows that Jesus had in mind the offering of Himself as the Passover Lamb. When He said to His disciples, 'Take and eat; this is my body,' He was offering them a share in His own life about to be broken on the cross for them.

As Christ's people, to recall who He was and what He said every time we break bread is to enter afresh into what our forefathers called 'the benefits of His atonement' and to renew our communion with Him. The theologian Dale Bruner says of the legacy of Jesus: 'Jesus did not want to leave His Church with only words ... He wanted to leave His Church with both His word and His touch, and so – to keep in touch – He wisely instituted the supper.' And as a great churchman of an earlier era, H.P. Liddon, commented: 'The sacraments are the guaranteed points of contact with the unseen Saviour.' They are!

Father, I am truly grateful for the wisdom of Your Son who bequeathed to us a meal that has so many wonderful and rich associations. Help me to get from it all that He put into it. In Jesus' name. Amen.

Why 'Good Friday'?

'This is my blood of the covenant, which is poured out for many for the forgiveness of sins.' (v28)

We come once again to Good Friday, the day which some say should be called 'Bad Friday' because of the awful and agonising crucifixion which Jesus had to endure on a Roman cross. We call it 'good' because though it was bad for Him it is good for us. What more pertinent and moving words could we contemplate on this day than those of Jesus when He said: 'This is my blood of the covenant, which is poured out for many for the forgiveness of sins'?

Biblically, blood is a vivid metaphor for a violent, sacrificial death. It is dramatic shorthand for the sacrifice of Jesus on the cross for the sins of the world. To those who have faith in Him His blood is precious and cleansing and life-giving. Derived from the Old Testament sacrificial system, such an image reminds us of the cost of our redemption, and that we have been bought with a price. Without the shedding of sacrificial blood there is no forgiveness of sins. The 'pouring out' of Christ's life-blood is a powerful image of self-sacrifice and evokes Isaiah's portrait of God's servant (see Isa. 53:12). We truly have forgiveness in His blood. In Ralph Turnbull's trenchant words: 'The goodwill announced in the Christmas gospel has been transmitted through the legacy "in Christ" and now confirmed in the last will and testament found in His Lord's Supper.'

This Easter time, may each of us, forgiven and restored, humbled and thankful, say with William Cowper:

> E'er since by faith, I saw the stream
> Thy flowing wounds supply,
> Redeeming love has been my theme,
> And shall be till I die.

FURTHER STUDY

Lev. 17:11;
Isa. 53:1-12;
Heb. 9:11-28

1. Why was it God's will to crush His Son?

2. Contrast the blood of animals with the blood of Christ.

Father, thank You for sending Your Son to die for me. Lord Jesus, thank You for giving Your life for me on that cross. Holy Spirit, thank You for making it all so real. Blessed Trinity, all honour and glory be to You for ever. Amen.

'Black Saturday'

FOR READING & MEDITATION - LUKE 22:20-30

'This cup is the new covenant in my blood, which is poured out for you.' (v20)

The Saturday following Good Friday, the day on which Jesus was crucified, has been called 'Black Saturday'. Jesus was dead and entombed, as if the dream was over. And there was much darkness abroad, from the moral and spiritual darkness in the betraying heart of Judas to the physical darkness that blacked out the sun and cast the shadow of death over the land (Matt. 27:45).

But against this black backdrop of sin and self-centredness the light shone ever more brightly. As the old, ugly story of human sin climaxed in the murderous rejection of God's Son, He was actually writing a new script in the story of God's covenant commitments. Remember, His is the blood of the *new* covenant. In this covenant, the very sinful hearts that have contrived His death may be amazingly transformed so as to further, and not sabotage, God's purposes. In this new covenant, long heralded by the prophets, sins are forgiven and forgotten, hard hearts are softened by grace to know the Lord and become disposed to do His will. By its provision, God's own Spirit will flood in to energise us to live in love, holiness and truthfulness. Where evil men do their worst, God does His best. And just as the old covenant was sealed with sacrificial blood so, too, is this new covenant – only this time with the very life-blood of the Messiah, God's Son, Jesus Christ.

FURTHER STUDY

Heb. 10:1-24

1. What has Christ's sacrifice made us?

2. What confidence does Christ's blood give us?

As you take bread and wine over this Easter season, seek to renew your faith in God's astonishing covenant commitment to us and to working within us. In God's name let us renounce the power-struggles that disfigure Christ's body, the Church, and humble ourselves to serve so that one day we may rule in the future kingdom.

Father, help me this Easter season to let go of everything that is not of You and to come to a deeper experience of personal renewal than ever before. In Jesus' name I ask it. Amen.

FOR READING & MEDITATION - MATTHEW 26:17-30

'I will not drink of this fruit of the vine ... until that day when I drink it anew with you in my Father's kingdom.' (v29)

It's Easter Day once again. Our Lord, once dead, is now gloriously alive. As all over the world Christians rejoice in this great fact, keep in mind it was Jesus' resurrection that changed the *Last* Supper into the *Lord's* Supper! But for the resurrection, the Last Supper would have literally been His last. Even in the upper room, the eyes of Jesus were turned towards the future when He will drink of the fruit of the vine anew with His disciples in His Father's kingdom. Because He died and rose again, everything has been made new: we have a new covenant, new life, and become a new creation (2 Cor. 5:17). We rejoice now in the life He gives and relish our hope of sharing in the final marriage supper of the Lamb (Rev. 19:7-9).

FURTHER STUDY

John 20:24-31; 1 Cor. 15:1-20

1. How are you referred to in Scripture?

2. What did Paul explain?

Meanwhile, for us, the Lord's Supper is never a funeral wake but always a feast of joy. Through the Holy Spirit's work, it is not so much Christ's absence but His real presence that makes our hearts long for His coming again. The bread and wine which we take are not the last rites of a lost cause but the first sacraments of a living Church. Jesus' disciples would have recalled the upper room on that dark night, but they would have recalled too those breakfasts and suppers eaten with Christ after He rose from the dead. They learned, as we do, that breaking bread with Him is not an act of commiseration but of communion with the once crucified but risen and returning Lord. As P.T. Forsyth asked: 'How can we have a mere memorial of One who is still alive, still our life, still present with us and acting in us?' In the words of Charles Wesley: 'Thus we remember Thee and take this bread and wine as Thine own dying legacy, and our redemption's sign.'

Father, thank You for reminding me on this Easter Day that when I participate in Holy Communion I am not engaging in a memorial but in a ministry - the ministry of One who died but lives again. Amen.

'In the midst'

FOR READING & MEDITATION - MATTHEW 18:15-20

'For where two or three come together in my name, there am I with them.' (v20)

The next legacy of our Lord we consider is that of His promises. The dictionary defines 'promise' as a vow made to assure someone that something will happen or be done. In the promise before us today our Lord assures us that whenever we meet in His name He is right there with us. It is important to notice that He does not say, 'I *will* be with them', but 'I *am* with them.' Whenever two or more believers meet in His name then He is there – automatically. He does not need to be invited – He just needs to be welcomed.

FURTHER STUDY

Mal. 3:16-18;
Heb. 13:1-8

1. What happens when we talk about the Lord?

2. What is our confidence?

This was revolutionary at a time when the Pharisees were seeking an alternative to the Temple as the place to meet God. They later stated: 'Where two or three gather around God's Torah, there is God's shekinah-glory.' Strikingly, Jesus puts His name in the place of God's law. If we meet on the basis of the authorised revelation of God that Jesus brought then we are assured of His presence as the risen Lord!

And there is more. 'I am with them' is wonderful enough. I am 'in the midst of them' (v20, AV) rightly implies that He is the focal point of His disciples' lives. Graham Scroggie, the Bible commentator, once said: 'A rose may be in the centre of the garden but its fragrance is in the midst; a lamp may be in the middle of the room but its light is in the midst!' Just as Jesus' presence is all pervasive, enveloping two friends, or a couple, while they converse, or walk, or pray together in His name. In Ian Macpherson's words: 'Christ is everywhere among us saturating the atmosphere like a lovely perfume … not in the centre (only) – but in the midst.'

Lord Jesus Christ, thank You for this wonderful and satisfying promise. Help me not only to remember it but also to celebrate it every time I meet with my brothers and sisters, whether it be with two or a hundred and two. Amen.

One thing is sure

FOR READING & MEDITATION - JOHN 14:1-14

'And if I go and prepare a place for you, I will come back and take you to be with me' (v3)

In the shadow of the cross, we might have expected the disciples to give Jesus emotional and spiritual support; instead He offers it *to them* in the form of the glorious promise we read in the words of our text for today. The words 'I will come back' have been taken as referring to His resurrection as they seem to do elsewhere in these farewell discourses (eg 14:18,28). To be sure, His 'going' involves going to the cross. But it also involves going to the Father to 'prepare a place' for His people, and so His promise here is best taken as a firm promise of His second coming.

Whatever the shape of the redeemed future, it is being carefully and lovingly prepared, and there is room in it for all God's faithful people. Above all, we will be wherever Christ is, and that surely will be joy for us all – a joy on which no shadow will ever descend. Of this splendid prospect, His appearances after death, risen and alive, are all the guarantee we need. And however indescribable the future is, we know it will be like going home.

There is even great comfort in the fact that Jesus said: 'If it were not so, I would have told you.' Jesus' honesty would not have allowed Him, while in full possession of the facts, to conceal anything from us. Being who He was, He simply had to tell the truth about what would happen in the days to come. He knows how desperately we long for a sure word concerning the curtained future. We may have varied anticipations of the future glory of the new world coming – some sharper than others. But we can all rest our troubled hearts and fix our trust on this rock-solid certainty: Jesus promised to return, and if it wasn't the case He would have told us!

FURTHER STUDY

1 Thess. 4:13-18; Rev. 21:1-7

1. How can we be encouraged about the future?

2. What does the future look like?

Father, there are some on whose word I cannot rely, but that cannot be said of You. I am certain that in all circumstances You tell the truth. You said You will return. I believe it. I receive it. And I await with great expectancy. Amen.

'Because He lives'

FOR READING & MEDITATION - JOHN 14:15-31

'Before long, the world will not see me any more, but you will see me.' (v19)

If yesterday's promise of Jesus' return – 'will come back' – refers to His second coming, today's – 'I will come to you' – almost certainly speaks of His return to His disciples after His resurrection. The context clearly supports this. Though Jesus is about to go away (in death), the disciples will once again see Him (v19). What a stunning promise this must have been but one wonders if they really took it in. They certainly understood it after His resurrection, but it is debatable whether they grasped the meaning of what He was saying when the words were uttered.

FURTHER STUDY

1 Thess. 5:1-11;
Rev. 22:1-14

1. What can we experience in life or death?

2. What right will God grant us?

We too can take heart from this promise. The Saviour knew that He would go through death and come out victorious on the other side. He would not simply be a resuscitated corpse, returning to His old mode of existence. He would enter into a new phase of existence, characterised by resurrection life and, in the reality of that new creation life, meet them again!

Many people, growing weary and cynical in our modern world, no longer ask 'Is there life after death?' but 'Is there life *before* death?' Jesus steps out from the other side of death to meet both conditions. He alone gives hope and substance to what lies beyond death in God's kingdom future. And He alone gives joy and meaning to the life to be lived before death in God's kingdom present. Whether now or then, in the perplexing present or uncertain future, He will not leave us as orphans. He will gather us to His Father and fold us in the loving embrace of His Father's family. On either side of death it remains true that He will come to us and that, because He lives, we shall live also, with the same quality of life He now enjoys!

Lord, You who have gone through death and come out again, how thankful I am that I am in You. Because of this I can never die. I close my eyes on earth to open them in heaven. What a prospect. Thank You Jesus. I am Yours for ever. Amen.

NEXT ISSUE

Revive us again

Revival shows us that God is able to do greater things than we have so far seen. But do we fully understand how revival is born of dependence on God?

In this issue, Selwyn explores the definition of revival as the return of the Church to the God-given norm of Pentecost. Reflect on your understanding of the Christlike power of the Holy Spirit; an extraordinary sense of God's holiness, and of renewed enthusiasm for prayer and reading Scripture as defining characteristics of revival.

Join us as we discover more of:
· God's sovereign action among believers
· God's call to repentance and dependency on Him
· Effective prayer for revival

Every Day with Jesus

MAY/JUN 2014

Revive us again

'For I will pour water on the thirsty land, and streams on the dry ground.'
Isaiah 44:3

Be revived and refreshed by God's Word   **CWR**

Also available as eBook/ eSubscription

Backed by the Godhead

FOR READING & MEDITATION - MATTHEW 28:16-20

'And surely I am with you always, to the very end of the age.' (v20)

Today we return to these final words of Jesus, this time to reflect on His promise to be with us *always*, to the end of the age. One problem we might have with this promise is that we can be so taken up with the excitement and thrill of His guaranteed presence with us to the end of the age that we overlook the extraordinary vision of Jesus this presents.

We have noted before the parallel to be drawn between the farewell speeches of Jesus and those of Moses. Such a comparison makes the contrasts all the more remarkable.

FURTHER STUDY

Matt. 1:18-25;
Mark 16:15-20

1. Why was the baby to be given specific names?

2. What was the experience of the disciples?

Moses, in his last message to the Israelites on the verge of entering Canaan, said, in effect: 'Go into the Promised Land, teaching and observing all that God has commanded you in His law, and God's presence will be with you always.' By contrast, Jesus says, 'Go into the promised *world*,' and instead of putting them under orders to teach what God has commanded He tells them to make disciples, 'teaching them to obey everything I have commanded you' (v20). Notice the phrase: 'I have commanded you.' Who is this person who makes such astounding claims and promises?

Who but Israel's God has the right to speak and act as He does? Who indeed! But then there is only one conclusion to be drawn: that the personal authority, truth and presence of the One Creator God is uniquely and indissolubly bound up with this person Jesus.

Once we make *that* move we can then go about our world mission not just with the memory of Jesus to spur us on but with the living presence of Jesus as 'God with us' (see Matt. 1:23) to accompany us. Jesus is God, and having Him we are backed by the entire Godhead.

Father, how reassuring it is to know that when I put my hand into the hand of Jesus I am in touch with the entire Godhead. If there is any lack it is only lack of trust. I believe, help me overcome my unbelief. In Jesus' name. Amen.

'The Divine Masterpiece'

FOR READING & MEDITATION – MATTHEW 16:13–20

'… on this rock I will build my church, and the gates of Hades will not overcome it.' (v18)

The promise we look at today is regarded by many as one of the greatest of all Jesus' promises. And not without good reason. The Amplified Bible translates verse 18: 'I will build my church and the gates of Hades (the powers of the infernal region) shall not overpower it – or be strong to its detriment, or hold out against it.'

Some ask: Will the Church survive the twenty-first century? Well, no one can guarantee the existence of the church building in which you worship, but when it comes to the body of the redeemed gathered from all the nations on earth then the answer is quite clear: it is unassailable and indestructible. Jesus has promised so. Let there be no further doubt: the Church is here to stay, both in time and in eternity.

The term 'Church' (*ekklesia* in the Greek) can stand in the New Testament, says one writer, for anything from 'a cosmic concourse to a congregational couple'. It can apply to the whole body of believers – some on earth and some in heaven – and also to a local group of Christians, which may consist of no more than two persons (see Matt. 18:20). The true Church of Jesus Christ is not a tall Gothic building with stained glass windows and surpliced clergy. That's the house in which the Church worships. The Church consists of men and women whose hearts have been washed in the blood of Christ.

One great Welsh preacher, Tom Rees, described the Church as 'The Divine Masterpiece'. Paul said in Ephesians 5:27 that one day Christ will present to Himself 'a radiant church, without stain or wrinkle or any other blemish'. Jesus will then contemplate His masterpiece with joy and delight for ever.

FURTHER STUDY

Eph. 3:1-21; 5:22-32

1. What was Paul's revelation?

2. How does Jesus feel about His church?

O Father, how consoling it is to rest on this promise that no matter how Your Church may be persecuted or oppressed, it is destined to exist for ever. You have promised so. I rest on that promise with joy and anticipation. Amen.

A night in prayer

FOR READING & MEDITATION - LUKE 6:12-16

'One of those days Jesus went out to a mountainside to pray,
and spent the night praying to God.' (v12)

Today we focus on yet another of Jesus' legacies – the men whom He chose to found His Church. Jesus spent a whole night in prayer before deciding who would become His disciples. Jesus prayed for many reasons, but this particular night of prayer was important not just because of what lay ahead but also because at the national level the choice of twelve disciples was significant and symbolic. He was reassigning His leadership of the twelve tribes of Israel to men of His choosing. And His new leaders were artisans, fishermen and men on the fringes of mainstream life.

FURTHER STUDY

Acts 4:1-22

1. What astonished the Sanhedrin?

2. How did the apostles respond to their threats?

This was a socially provocative gesture, demonstrating that He had the goal and authority to rebuild the life of the people of God under His lordship. At a personal level, the twelve must have been astonished (whether then or later) to find themselves promised such exalted status in the future restoration of Israel (see Matt. 19:28). We cannot be certain that the disciples knew at the moment of their choosing that their selection had been based on a night of prayer (clearly they knew it later or it would not be contained in the sacred record). But if it was conveyed to them at the time, how it must have nourished them at a deep level to know they had been handpicked by Jesus after prayerful consultation with His heavenly Father.

Our sense of privilege need be no less than theirs. 'In Christ' we too have been chosen from before the world's foundations (see Eph. 1:4), the object of the loving communion of the eternal Father and Son. Our mission, like theirs, flows out of His love; betrayals like that of Judas occur when we lose touch with such a love.

O God my heavenly Father, once again my heart rejoices to know that I was chosen not by whim but by Your predetermined will in eternity. You sought me, bought me, and now I am Yours for ever. How wonderful. Amen.

A curious mixture

FOR READING & MEDITATION - ACTS 1:12-26

'Those present were Peter, John, James and Andrew; Philip and
Thomas, Bartholomew and Matthew' (v13)

We continue reflecting on the men whom Christ appointed
to establish His Church and continue the work He
began. When you think of it, Jesus took an enormous risk
in entrusting the future to these men. What a motley bunch
they were. Take just four examples. There was Peter who
was hot-headed, impulsive, impetuous, and something of a
boaster. What a curious mixture he was – able to walk on the
water to Jesus (Matt. 14:28–29) and yet we read he 'followed
at a distance' on the land (Luke 22:54). Then there was John.
He was Peter's psychological opposite as he was a mystical
man of deep thought, an introspective soul, rapt
in perpetual contemplation. Then again there was
Andrew, a man who loved to work behind the
scenes and do what he could for the cause without
blatantly advertising his activities. Every time we
see Andrew in the Gospels he is bringing someone
to Jesus. Finally take Thomas, *doubting* Thomas as
we sometimes call him. He was the rationalist of
the party, a hard-headed, shrewd man who carried
his faith at his fingertips, so to speak. In these four
men we have represented the four points of the
psychological compass, yet they were taken by Christ and
moulded into men who became invincible.

**FURTHER
STUDY**

Eph. 1:1-14;
2:6-10

1. Why did Jesus
choose us?

2. For what
have we been
chosen?

Brennan Manning says: 'Christ's reaction to their
broken, inconsistent discipleship was one of unending
love.' This mixed bunch, who would never have chosen
each other, were together because Jesus had chosen them
and continued to love them despite their flaws. Now, as He
ascended to heaven, He risked all in entrusting the mission
to them because He had total confidence in the work He
had left with them and, of course, in the empowerment of
the Spirit they were soon to receive.

**Father, I see that a society that can use a Peter, an Andrew, a
John and a Thomas as one team is no ordinary society. It is a
society which has at its head a Master who can change things. I
am so glad I am part of that society. Amen.**

God's holy army

FOR READING & MEDITATION - EPHESIANS 4:1-16

'... he ... gave some to be apostles, some to be prophets, some to be evangelists, and some to be pastors and teachers' (v11)

Having spent a few days considering the fact that one of Christ's legacies to us was the original disciples (later called apostles) who were used by the Holy Spirit to establish the Church, we should not overlook the fact that through them He set in motion a constant stream of ministries to build up His Church – apostles, prophets, pastors, teachers, and evangelists. Some believe the apostles and prophets dropped away once the Church was established in the first century and that now the Church runs only on pastors, teachers, and evangelists. This is not the place to embark upon a defence of modern-day apostles and prophets, but it is my conviction that though the original apostles were given a special foundational work to achieve, the apostolic and prophetic ministries, though often unrecognised, still function in the Church of today.

FURTHER STUDY

Rom. 12:1-8;
1 Cor. 12:12-31

1. List the different roles in Christ's body.

2. Why are 'invisible' people necessary?

It is interesting to note that the quotation from Psalm 68:18, found in verse 8, is slightly altered by Paul from 'you received gifts from men' to 'he ... gave gifts to men.' The gifts Christ gives to the Church are 'captives' – captured rebels like Paul himself – whom Jesus wins and conquers and turns round as part of His holy army.

Each of these ministries – that of apostle, prophet, evangelist, pastor, teacher – represent facets of Jesus' own ministry. He Himself was every one of these. But no one person can truly represent Jesus. So He divides up His unique and full ministry and distributes grace to different members of His body (v7). Together, working as one, united as a team, these different ministries are designed to bring the fullness of Christ to the Church, and the fullness of the Church to Christ.

Father, we give thanks to You today for all we owe to those whom Jesus bequeathed to us for our growth and development in Him. In Jesus' name. Amen.

Why Jesus never wrote a book

FOR READING & MEDITATION - JOHN 8:1-11

'Again he stooped down and wrote on the ground.' (v8)

As we draw our meditations on 'The Great Legacy' to a close it needs to be clear that we have not exhausted the subject by any means. Other matters we could have included are the example Jesus left us in His prayer life, His relational style, His love for children, the manner in which He witnessed to the Father, and His teaching methods.

Throughout the ages people have raised the question: Since Jesus Christ had so much to offer humanity why didn't He write a book? How we would have valued an autobiography. In fact, the only mention of Jesus writing is found in the passage before us today. He wrote, we are told, in the sand, but what He wrote has been lost, blown away by the winds. The great Dr W.E. Sangster once pointed out that if Jesus had left us a book written by His own hand it might have become venerated as an icon and become the object of idolatrous worship. But, though Jesus never wrote a book, He inspired men to write the four Gospels and also the epistles so that through them we might have an understanding of His last will and testament. Jesus promised that the Holy Spirit would lead them into all truth, would show them the things that were to come, and would glorify Him.

FURTHER STUDY

John 20:30-31;
2 Tim. 3:14-17;
1 John 1:1-4

1. What is the purpose of Scripture?

2. Why did John write his letters?

Perhaps the New Testament itself should be regarded as the first result of that promise. The preacher P.T. Forsyth once memorably described the New Testament letters as the 'posthumous epistles of the ascended Christ'. In this profound sense, the New Testament is the book that Jesus never wrote. He has bequeathed His testimony to us in every page of the New Testament. It is essentially the autobiography of Jesus.

Father, how thankful I am for the insight and enlightenment that comes to me through the writings of the men You inspired. You have gone into their words and You are revealed by them. I am so grateful. Amen.

The whole estate

FOR READING & MEDITATION - 1 CORINTHIANS 3:18-23
'All things are yours ...' (v.21)

What an appropriate text with which to end our meditations. If any verse of Scripture sounds like the reading of a last will and testament, this does! Jesus has inherited the whole of His Father's estate. But He never keeps anything for Himself. He always shares it with us!

'When Christ left the world,' said the commentator Matthew Henry, 'He made His will. His soul He bequeathed to His Father, His body to Joseph of Arimathea, His clothes fell to the soldiers, and His mother He left to the care of John, the beloved disciple.' His was a negligible legacy so far as material possessions were concerned but, as Ian Macpherson reminds us: 'He bequeathed the whole universe to those who belong to him.' All ministries that truly proclaim Christ are ours. All human experience is ours – we possess it; it does not possess us! In Christ we even own death; it does not *possess* us! We possess, too, the future even if we do not know what it holds. And the present is ours as well. The gift of life today which enables you to read these notes is something to be wondered at and cherished and, as far as is possible, enjoyed. Only one thing does not belong to us – *ourselves*. Once we give ourselves to Jesus Christ then we belong to Him – for ever. We are no longer our own; we are His. At conversion we give up the little we own – ourselves – and lo, we end up with everything!

FURTHER STUDY

Rom. 8:28-39;
1 Cor. 6:19-20

1. What is our relationship with the Creator and creation?

2. Do Christians have a right of self-determination?

Let the last word be with the modern-day Christian martyr Jim Elliot: 'He is no fool who gives up what he cannot keep in order to gain what he cannot lose.' In possessing nothing, we own all things; penniless, we own the world. Hallelujah!

My Father and my God, surrounded by the riches that You have bequeathed to me I will never again complain of what I lack. In You I have everything. Everything! All honour and glory be to Your peerless name for ever. Amen.

ORDER FORM

4 EASY WAYS TO ORDER:

1. Phone in your credit card order: **01252 784710** (Mon-Fri, 9.30am - 5pm)

2. Visit our Online Store at **www.cwr.org.uk/store**

3. Send this form together with your payment to:
   CWR, Waverley Abbey House, Waverley Lane, Farnham, Surrey GU9 8EP

4. Visit your local Christian bookshop

a list of our National Distributors, who supply countries outside the UK, visit www.cwr.org.uk/distributors

YOUR DETAILS (REQUIRED FOR ORDERS AND DONATIONS)

Full name: _____   CWR ID No. (if known): _____

Home Address: _____

Postcode: _____

Telephone No. (for queries): _____   Email: _____

PUBLICATIONS

TITLE	QTY	PRICE	TOTAL
		Total publications	

All CWR adult Bible-reading notes are also available in ebook and email subscription format.
Visit www.cwr.org.uk for further information.

UK p&p: up to £24.99 = **£2.99**; £25.00 and over = **FREE**

Elsewhere p&p: up to £10 = **£4.95**; £10.01 - £50 = **£6.95**; £50.01 - £99.99 = **£10**; £100 and over = **£30**

Please allow 14 days for delivery   **Total publications and p&p A** [ ]

SUBSCRIPTIONS* (NON DIRECT DEBIT)

	QTY	PRICE (INCLUDING P&P)			TOTAL
		UK	Europe	Elsewhere	
Every Day with Jesus (1yr, 6 issues)		£15.95	£19.95	Please contact nearest National Distributor or CWR direct	
Large Print Every Day with Jesus (1yr, 6 issues)		£15.95	£19.95		
Inspiring Women Every Day (1yr, 6 issues)		£15.95	£19.95		
Life Every Day (Jeff Lucas) (1yr, 6 issues)		£15.95	£19.95		
Cover to Cover Every Day (1yr, 6 issues)		£15.95	£19.95		
Mettle: 14-18s (1yr, 3 issues)		£14.50	£16.60		
YP's: 11-15s (1yr, 6 issues)		£15.95	£19.95		
Topz: 7-11s (1yr, 6 issues)		£15.95	£19.95		
Total Subscriptions (Subscription prices already include postage and packing) **B**					

Please circle which bimonthly issue you would like your subscription to commence from:
Jan/Feb Mar/Apr May/Jun Jul/Aug Sep/Oct Nov/Dec

Only use this section for subscriptions paid for by credit/debit card or
cheque. For Direct Debit subscriptions see overleaf.

CONTINUED OVERLEAF >>

PAYMENT DETAILS

☐ I enclose a cheque/PO made payable to CWR for the amount of: **£** _____

☐ Please charge my credit/debit card.

Cardholder's name (in BLOCK CAPITALS) _____

Card No. ☐☐☐☐ ☐☐☐☐ ☐☐☐☐ ☐☐☐☐

Expires end ☐☐ ☐☐   Security Code ☐☐☐

GIFT TO CWR   ☐ Please send me an acknowledgement of my gift   **C** ☐

GIFT AID (YOUR HOME ADDRESS REQUIRED, SEE OVERLEAF)

giftaid it

I am a UK taxpayer and want CWR to reclaim the tax on all my donations for the four years prior to this year **and on** all donations I make from the date of this Gift Aid declaration until further notice.*

Taxpayer's Full Name (in BLOCK CAPITALS) _____

Signature _____ **Date** _____

*I understand I must pay an amount of Income/Capital Gains Tax at least equal to the tax the charity reclaims in the tax year.

GRAND TOTAL (Total of A, B, & C) ☐

SUBSCRIPTIONS BY DIRECT DEBIT (UK BANK ACCOUNT HOLDERS ONLY)

Subscriptions cost £15.95 (except *Mettle*: £14.50) for one year for delivery within the UK. Please tick relevant boxes and fill in the form

☐ *Every Day with Jesus* (1yr, 6 issues)
☐ Large Print *Every Day with Jesus* (1yr, 6 issues)
☐ *Inspiring Women Every Day* (1yr, 6 issues)
☐ *Life Every Day* (Jeff Lucas) (1yr, 6 issues)

☐ *Cover to Cover Every Day* (1yr, 6 issues)
☐ *Mettle*: 14-18s (1yr, 3 issues)
☐ *YP's*: 11-15s (1yr, 6 issues)
☐ *Topz*: 7-11s (1yr, 6 issues)

Issue to commence
☐ Jan/Feb ☐ Jul/Aug
☐ Mar/Apr ☐ Sep/Oct
☐ May/Jun ☐ Nov/De

CWR

Instruction to your Bank or Building Society to pay by Direct Debit

DIRECT Debit

Please fill in the form and send to: CWR, Waverley Abbey House, Waverley Lane, Farnham, Surrey GU9 8EP

Name and full postal address of your Bank or Building Society

To: The Manager   Bank/Building Society

Address _____

Postcode _____

Name(s) of Account Holder(s)

Branch Sort Code ☐☐ ☐☐ ☐☐

Bank/Building Society account number ☐☐☐☐☐☐☐☐

Originator's Identification Number

4	2	0	4	8	7

Reference ☐☐☐☐☐☐☐☐☐☐☐

Instruction to your Bank or Building Society

Please pay CWR Direct Debits from the account detailed in this Instruction s to the safeguards assured by the Direct Debit Guarantee.
I understand that this Instruction may remain with CWR and, if so, details will passed electronically to my Bank/Building Society.

Signature(s) _____

Date _____

Banks and Building Societies may not accept Direct Debit Instructions for some types of account